NURTURING GIRLPOWER

Integrating eating disorder
prevention/intervention
skills into your practice.

by
Sandra Susan Friedman
BA, BSW, MA

SALAL BOOKS

Vancouver
British Columbia
Canada

National Library of Canada Cataloguing in Publication

Friedman, Sandra Susan, 1942-
    Nurturing girlpower: integrating eating disorder prevention/intervention skills into your practice / by Sandra Susan Friedman. --2nd ed.

Includes bibliographical references.
ISBN 0-9698883-4-1

    1. Eating disorders in adolescence--Prevention. 2. Teenage girls--Mental health. I. Title.

    HQ798.F74 2003   616.85'2605'08352   C2003-905015-7

Cover design by Leon Phillips   www.leonphillips.ca

Text editing & DTP production by Dan Fivehouse for:
SALAL BOOKS
#309, 101-1184 Denman Street
Vancouver, British Columbia, Canada   V6G 2M9
☎ + 604-689-8399   www.salal.com

Printing:
FRIESENS Corporation
One Printers Way
Altona, Manitoba, Canada   R0G 0B0
☎ 204-324-6401   204-324-1333   www.friesens.com

Second edition: September 2003

ACKNOWLEDGEMENTS

NURTURING GIRLPOWER evolved out of a series of prevention and intervention workshops that I developed and facilitated in British Columbia for *Eating Disorders Project North*. I would like to thank Dr. Lorna Medd, project manager and Chief Medical Health Officer for Northern Interior Health Authority, for inviting me to be a part of this project.

Thanks to my colleagues on the project and to all the participants in training sessions in Prince George, Terrace and Dawson Creek. Thanks also to all those who have taken part in other workshops that I have facilitated across Canada and the United States. It has been an honor for me to be a part of your lives and to learn from your willingness to share your feelings, experiences and opinions. The heated discussions were great!

Many, many thanks to the women who took the time to review this book in manuscript form and give me feedback: Arlene Carlson and Tara Case from Prince Rupert; Charlotte Tooms and Karla Hennig and Anne Pelletier and Darlene Westerman from Terrace; and Jerrilyn Rochon from Tumbler Ridge. They all shared a unique perspective as former participants in Eating Disorders Project North. Joanne Houghton and Raine McKay shared their expertise and experiences with community development. Jackie Abbott of Portland, Oregon, provided me with value information about nutrition.

My colleagues in prevention went over the manuscript with a fine-toothed comb thereby enriching the manual as well as providing me with food for thought. Anita Romaniw; Community Nutritionist for the Fraser Valley Health Authority in British Columbia; Lori Irving, Associate Professor of Psychology at Washington State University in Vancouver, Washington; Merryl Bear, Executive Director of NEDIC (National Eating Disorder Information Centre) in Toronto, Ontario; and Sharon Young, Health Promotion Educator with the Brandon Regional Health Authority in Manitoba, advised on the first edition. Ann Kerr and Jane Koh from Sheena's Place in Toronto read the new chapters on eating disorders and on prevention and Meris Williams commented on the chapter on intervention.

Thanks to Tammy Lawrence, former Executive Director of proMOTION plus; Michael Levine of Kenyon College; Valerie Edwards and the rest of the Columbia River Eating Disorder Network and Bill Coleman and my colleagues on the Canadian Coalition to End Disordered Eating Network for keeping me up to date with interesting articles and data. Thanks to Sotiria Tsirigotis for teaching me about the role of leisure in physical activity.

As always, my heartfelt thanks to my husband and editor and publisher Dan Fivehouse for his superb talents and continuing support in all of my endeavors.

TABLE OF CONTENTS

INTRODUCTION

It is difficult to grow up female today without ever dieting or experiencing some form of disordered eating. Eating disorders rank as the third major chronic health risk to girls. Since the 1950s anorexia nervosa has been increasing by 36% every five years.[1] Three out of every one hundred girls will develop anorexia nervosa or bulimia—often in the wake of puberty.[2] Thirteen percent of teenage girls (although not yet diagnosed with full-blown eating disorders) engage in anorectic and bulimic behaviors such as self-induced vomiting, skipping meals, abuse of laxatives and diet pills, and cycles of binge eating and dieting.[3]

The dramatic increase in eating disorders are a result of the same environmental and social factors that make girls vulnerable to other risks—depression, smoking, teen pregnancy and sexually transmitted diseases—stemming from a loss of girlpower.

Girls with *girlpower*

➢ Can express their feelings constructively.

➢ Are able to set boundaries.

➢ Have healthy connections with others.

➢ Develop their self-esteem in areas other than looking good.

➢ Have a good sense of their bodies.

➢ Are physically active.

➢ Have a healthy relationship with food.

NURTURING GIRLPOWER: *Integrating Eating Disorder Prevention and Intervention Skills into Your Practice* evolved out of my work with *Eating Disorders Project North* 1999 to 2000. The project built capacity so that communities in northern British Columbia could address prevention, intervention, psychological treatment and medical diagnosis and management at the local level. I developed and facilitated the three-day workshops on prevention and on intervention.

---

[1] S. Willard, De Paul Tulane Hospital in *Dying to be Thin* video, Nova, December 12, 2000. Larking McPhee, director

[2] Willard in *Dying to be Thin*

[3] J.D.Killen, C.B.Taylor, M.J.Telch, K.E.Saylor, D.J. Moaron, & T.N. Robinson. "Self-induced vomiting, laxative and diuretic use among teenagers: Precursors of the binge-purge syndrome," *Journal of the American Medical Association*, 255:1442-1449, 1986

This manual draws upon the professional skills of my lifetime of practice as a teacher, as a psychotherapist working with girls and women with eating disorders and issues around food and weight, and through my work developing programs and facilitating professional training workshops concerned with eating disorder prevention/ intervention, addressing childhood obesity and getting girls physically active.

In 1992 I developed JUST FOR GIRLS, a group discussion program that made girls aware of their *grungies*—a term coined to describe 'feeling fat' and other aspects of their negative voice. It encourages them to tell the real stories that lie underneath their behavior and teaches them to substitute healthy self-expression for self-repression. The companion book WHEN GIRLS FEEL FAT: *Helping Girls Through Adolescence* (1997, 2000) was written originally for mothers and other mentors who wanted additional information and to develop skills for their own use, but it continues to be a popular read among girls themselves. BODY THIEVES: *Help Girls Reclaim Their Natural Bodies and Become Physically Active* (2002) addresses eating disorder prevention, the current crisis of childhood obesity, and how to get girls physically active. Descriptions of these publications can be found at the end of this manual.

This second edition of NURTURING GIRLPOWER: *Integrating Eating Disorder Prevention and Intervention Skills into Your Practice* integrates further experience and learning on my part. The manual is women-centered, because most of the participants in my professional training workshops are women and it is mainly females who develop eating disorders. It models the relational and contextual way in which many girls and women learn, and how we should in turn work with them. The information and skills are linked with practical applications. There are tests you can use with girls (try them out by yourself first), and learning activities. This manual can also be used by men who want to expand their knowledge of female culture and try out new ways of working with girls or adapt the information to their work with boys.

NURTURING GIRLPOWER is based upon the belief that disordered eating, eating disorders, and certain other health and social risks are coping mechanisms girls develop in order to deal with feelings and situations for which they have no other means of expression—especially the challenges of adolescence and the changes in their bodies and their lives. Prevention is about promoting and sustaining positive healthy development— nurturing girlpower. Intervention means stopping the behaviors girls experiment with before they develop into eating disorders and/or restoring girlpower that is in danger of being lost.

The material in this manual is structured for cumulative, incremental learning. That means there is an underlying logic and there will be a certain amount of repetition of concepts. It begins with a theoretical framework based upon gender and development to help you understand what happens to girls (and boys) as they grow, and the effects of societal pressures upon them.

The next section provides you with basic information about eating disorders—including compulsive exercise and muscle dysmorphia in boys and men. *Prevention* presents a comprehensive framework for addressing eating disorder prevention. *Implementing Prevention Strategies* helps you incorporate basic elements of prevention in your individual practice, provides you with check lists to assess prevention practices in your schools, helps you create a body-friendly environment in your community and helps you develop and evaluate community strategies and network teams of local practitioners.

Once you have a firm understanding of prevention, *Acquiring Prevention Skills* provides you with information and strategies to address the particular issues that arise from the physical changes in girls' bodies, and the issues that arise from the behavioral changes in their lives. These include decoding the 'language of fat' by teaching girls about the *grungies* (their negative voice), developing body image awareness, teaching communication skills, understanding the myths and prejudice around fat, empowering girls who are fat, getting girls physically active, the effects of dieting, dealing with stress, teaching media literacy and activism, and addressing the issue of bullying. Much of the material presented in this section can also be adapted for intervention, and to address childhood obesity and for use with boys. The following section helps you apply prevention skills to classroom lessons, to teachable moments and to presentations for elementary/middle and secondary school girls. It describes how to organize and structure a *Girls' Day* and provides basic information about working with groups.

NURTURING GIRLPOWER then moves on to intervention. This section helps you demystify eating disorders by breaking down the dynamics and behaviors into small components so that you can better relate to the girl instead of her disorder. It helps you understand how eating disorders develop within a social context as well as within the more intimate context of the realities of girls' lives and experiences. It presents the Golden Rule of Counseling as well as basic counseling skills.

NURTURING GIRLPOWER is designed for use by women (and interested men) coming from diverse orientations and differing levels of experience. You don't need four PhDs to practice eating disorder prevention and intervention. You should find that you are dealing with material that you can already relate to for working with girls with whom you already have some connection. What you need is a lot of personal curiosity, the ability to listen to the voices of girls, the ability to share yourself and a willingness to try out different approaches to things. As one participant in the Eating Disorders Project North workshops taught us, practice doesn't make perfect—it makes improvement. A sense of humor also helps!

BUILDING THE FRAMEWORK

It is impossible to grow up female today without ever worrying about weight or feeling fat. Dieting has become the national pastime as little girls watch their mothers and copy what they do. Six and seven year old girls express concern with how they look. Nine year old girls talk about wanting to be thinner even before their bodies have begun to undergo the changes of puberty. Fat prejudice is at an all time high. Eating disorders now rank as the third chronic health risk to girls and they are beginning to affect boys.

In order to prevent eating disorders and to intervene with girls who have begun to experiment with the behaviors, we need to know what happens to them in the process of growing up that silences their voices and transfers so much of their self-esteem and self worth onto how they look. We need to know what happens to boys that make them want to bulk up or to reduce their body size in order to feel strong in their lives. We need to understand society and the role that it plays in shaping who we are. The framework that provides the foundation for our understanding and upon which this book is built is that of gender and development.

GENDER AND DEVELOPMENT

Sex refers to the biological differences between males and females including anatomy (such as body size and conformation), and physiology (such as hormonal activity and organ functioning). *Gender* refers to the array of socially constructed roles and relationships, personality traits, attitudes, behaviors, values, and relative power that society ascribes to the two different sexes. Gender teaches us how to act and behave separately as girls and boys and later as women and men. In fact, as girls and boys grow up they inhabit two different gender cultures using different languages and with different ways of interpreting and responding to the world.

As you read this section please keep in mind I am using generalities and describing averages. If you or someone you know doesn't fit the descriptions, don't panic! While we as individuals share many characteristics that are common to our specific gender we also occupy varying places on the continuum of human behavior.

Differences Begin in the Womb

For the first six or seven weeks after conception all fetuses develop along female lines and appear the same. Then chemical messengers in the form of sex hormones (steroids called androgens and estrogens) ensure the designated male/female genetic programs are carried out. A fetus that is destined to be female develops cells that produce and bath it in *estrogen*. By the thirteenth week of gestation gonads appear in the form of ovaries. These produce tiny amounts of testosterone that influence the development of the female brain.

In fetuses that are genetically male the male androgen *testosterone* stimulates the development of male genitalia. Testosterone interacts with the nerve cells (neurons) that make up the brain and stimulates dramatic changes that alter the brain from one that is female into one that is distinctly male.

Basic differences in brain structure account for many of the differences in behavior in boys and girls. These differences become evident shortly after birth. Girl babies show a tendency to be interested in people and communication. Even when they are as young as two to four days old girls pay attention longer than boys do when adults are speaking and spend almost twice as long maintaining eye contact. They are more tuned in to facial expressions and emotional nuances and will lose interest once the connection is broken. The female brain responds more intensely to emotion. Feelings, especially sadness, activate neurons in an area eight times larger in the female brain than in the male. Even before they can understand language, girls seem to be better at identifying the emotional content of speech.

Boys tend to be interested in dynamic activity and in objects. Male babies will continue to jabber away at toys long after the adult has ended the contact. Boys are more active and wakeful than girls, more sensitive to bright light and focus more on depth perception and perspective than on the wider picture. Because the male brain is more compartmentalized than the female brain boys can focus more intensely on doing one thing well. They are task-oriented because their brain turns on and off between tasks. Their attention span and motor activity are shorter than those of girls but are made up of more intensely active periods. They have better hand/eye coordination and better spatial relations.

It is important to remember neither brain structure is superior to the other. Nor are girls and boys restricted in what they can do. Because different parts of the brain grow at different times and at different rates, girls and boys acquire certain skills at different times. As well, the ways they learn to perform these skills are different and are influenced by their environment and the society in which we live.

THE STORY OF *GRIT*—THE PROTOTYPICAL BOY

I have named the prototypical boy **GRIT** because he is **G**oal-oriented (or task-oriented), **R**ational, **I**ndependent and **T**ough. In order to understand how he became that way, we need to understand male psychological development, male gender culture and the influence of society on his behavior.

Many psychological theorists see male development as occurring in progressive stages. They believe boys must separate from their mothers in order to develop a male identity that is based upon becoming independent and standing on their own two feet. (There is much debate today about the necessity of making this separation at a very early age because of the harmful psychological cost to boys.) Psychological theories also hold that boys develop their sense-of-self based upon their individual accomplishments and how well they perform in the world.

Recent literature about boys describe them as growing up with tremendous energy and exuberance, a willingness to venture into the unknown, to take action, and a need to test their limits. Boys tend to play in groups where they can exercise their need for physical activity and for controlling their territory. Team sports teach them about winning and losing and being on top. Boys are able to deal with and depersonalize conflict better than girls. When boys enter into new situations they measure themselves in terms of their sense of adequacy and where they fit in. Loyalty and fairness play a big part in boys' friendships. They support each other by diffusing emotional intensity and cheering each other up. Boys feel most comfortable with interpersonal communication when it takes place in the context of an activity or when boys are side-by-side rather than face-to-face. Boys tend to solve problems on their own rather than make themselves vulnerable by consulting someone else.

The Impact of Society on Male Development

As infants, boys are more emotionally expressive, more sensitive and cry more easily than girls. By the time boys are around five years old, however, they are pressured to close down the relational half of their emotional range. Being male is defined as oppositional to traditional female qualities—as *not being* female. While it is all right to be a 'Daddy's girl', 'Mama's boys' are sissies. Society prepares boys to become men by 'toughening them up' and disciplining them through the use of shame. From the first day of kindergarten boys are expected to measure up to other boys, to show that they are 'real' boys—and real boys don't cry.

The Trauma of Adolescence

Boys experience immense pressure to conform to a rigid ideal of masculinity that is action-oriented and focuses on physical prowess and achievement in external, measurable activities. Because boys are encouraged to repress all of their feelings except for anger and rage, they learn to detach from their own experiences and to ignore or 'suck up' fear and pain. Boys who are 'cool' keep their feelings of hurt and anxiety and inadequacy bottled up inside. They act tough, hide their empathy, and laugh their feelings off.

Adolescent boys enforce the code of masculinity on one another through a culture of cruelty. Boys who don't measure up are bullied by their peers and are called *fag, wuss* and *girl*. The code of masculinity prevents boys who are going through puberty from sharing their fears and concerns over their changing bodies and the numerous hormonal surges they experience. Lacking adequate information, many boys feel these changes are not normal and they will never measure up as men. Because intimacy is discouraged in early development, it only enters into the male developmental scheme during adolescence. Boys learn to associate intimacy with sexuality, and because of the emphasis on male performance, boys who long for intimacy often become sexual adventurers instead.

During adolescence many boys split into two selves. The inner self contains the feelings that society teaches boys are unacceptable—feelings such as loneliness, insecurity, fear and affection and attachment. The outer self reflects the image of male toughness and emotional detachment our society defines as strength. Boys hide their vulnerability behind a mask of bravado. As they lose touch with their feelings, the inner self becomes buried and the mask becomes the only sense of self that they know or understand.

How Boys Deal with Societal Pressures

Most boys are socialized to externalize distress. They react to situations by imagining themselves unfairly treated by others and thus transform their feelings into anger and blame which they direct outward. ("He made me do it." "It's your fault that I am angry.") Boys may also deal with distress through the use of alcohol and drugs and action-oriented risk-taking behavior.

Many boys internalize their real distress. They try to solve problems on their own because asking for help is a loss of face. The depression many of them experience is often undetected because they are socialized to hide their pain and are shamed into not complaining. While a greater number of girls attempt suicide, more boys succeed.

Boys today are under increasing pressure to value themselves in terms of how they look. The hard body and well-developed muscles of the 'ideal' man reinforces society's image of masculinity. Boys who are teased about being fat often begin to diet. Boys who feel thin, awkward and inadequate and who have been teased about their bodies try to bulk up in order to gain an illusion of control in their lives. They associate the well-built muscular body with fame, respect, power and sex appeal. They exercise, become obsessed with their looks, and attempt to control their weight in much the same way girls do. Boys who want to improve their performance in sports and/or change how they look may use anabolic steroids in an attempt to make their bodies bigger.

THE STORY OF *RICA*—THE PROTOTYPICAL GIRL

RICA is the prototypical female because she is **R**elational, **I**nterdependent, **C**ontextual and **A**ccommodating. Research on female development indicates girls do not separate from their mothers but instead develop their identities in the context of that relationship and through their relationships with subsequent important people in their lives. Girls are *inter*dependent. Put into practice, girls travel in pairs. [How many girls go into the bathroom in company with one another?]

The relational and contextual perspective girls develop forms the basis of their female gender culture. It influences how they learn, the stories they tell and the ways they tell them, what they think is important and how they get things done. Girls tend to play in small groups that are based upon communication and connection. Their games teach them empathy and sensitivity and have fewer rules than boys' games. Girls often change the rules to accommodate situations as they arise. Girls have a best friend. They tell each other secrets. They use language to negotiate relationships and to create intimacy. They do this through sharing the details of their lives. Girls solve problems by talking to a friend. If it's a big problem, they'll talk to two friends. Their perception of adequacy is based upon the degree of connection they have with others rather than on performance as it is in boys.

The Impact of Society on Female Development

Before girls reach adolescence, they tend to thrive in their female gender culture. They are physically active and relatively unselfconscious about their bodies. They speak their minds and voice their opinions. Because they mature faster than boys, they can read and write at an earlier age and have a longer attention span. They are taller than boys are and are physically stronger—because they weigh more. They are just as active as boys. Their behavior is relatively unrestricted from societal pressure.

Changes in Girls' Bodies

As their bodies begin to change during puberty, many girls disengage from their inner and/or kinesthetic experience and begin to focus largely on their external appearance—on how they look to others. Because of our society's emphasis on thinness as a measure of worth and value, many girls believe their accumulation of body fat (which is biologically normal and necessary to female development) is abnormal. Girls measure themselves against each other and reinforce the message they must constantly try to change their bodies to fit in. At a time when they need the most nourishment, many girls begin restricting their food intake in fear of getting fat.

As girls get their menstrual periods, fluctuating hormones and PMS can make them feel out of control. Their lack of adequate information concerning female development makes them feel there is something wrong with them. Because girls begin puberty at different times, they can feel out of step with their peers. Some must deal with teasing they receive because they mature early. Others must deal with the angst of being a late bloomer—being the only one who doesn't yet have breasts. During puberty many girls stop using their bodies because they feel self-conscious about them. They become critical of their bodies and try to change them.

Girls who experience sexism, racism, homophobia and weight prejudice turn their feelings against themselves and feel shame. Instead of being angry with the source, they feel something is wrong with their bodies and with themselves.

Sexual harassment and objectification also intensify the process by which girls disconnect from their bodies. When boys and men make comments about girls' bodies, girls come to feel their bodies are not their own. Sexual harassment begins in the elementary schools as a form of bullying. Because of the influence of video games and rap music, boys and girls learn to call girls *sluts*, *whores*, (or *hos*), *cunts* and *bitches*. Boys pinch girls' breasts, lift their skirts and thrust their hands between girls' legs. When sexual harassment is not stopped, it escalates. Many girls can't walk down the hall in high school without being grabbed and groped. They often don't feel safe when they participate in class because being 'seen' makes them vulnerable to undesirable attention from boys.

Changes in Girls' Lives

Girls develop their identity in the context of their relationships—first with their mothers and then with other significant people in their lives. Because their self-esteem is tied to the success of their social skills, they flourish when their relationships are open, honest and mutually supportive.

When girls reach adolescence, adult society (people such as us) tells girls it is better to be *kind* and *nice* and 'not hurt anyone's feelings' than to be honest and say what they really think and feel. This places girls in a terrible dilemma. If they are honest they will be shunned by other girls and will jeopardize their relationships. If they are *kind* and *nice* (and therefore hold back their feelings and opinions) they will lose touch with who they are, how they feel and what is important to them. They will also lose their real connections with others.[*]

Girls begin to hold back their feelings and opinions in order to fit into their peer group and conform to these expectations of society. They learn the way to stay close is to hide

---

[*] The 'tyranny of kind and nice' was first described by Carol Gilligan.

parts of themselves. The fear of hurting someone else or of not being liked leaves them with no way to deal directly with anger and conflict. Not only are their friendships profoundly altered, they also take on a dark side. Girls tease and bully each other. They develop secrets. They form cliques. They learn alliances are temporary and elusive and that it is not safe to be direct.

Because of societal pressure to please others, girls have a difficult time with boundaries. They are afraid if they say 'no' they will be rejected and if they say 'yes' they will be seen as selfish. Girls who become interested in boys may have sex when they don't really want to, or have unsafe sex because they don't want to hurt the boy's feelings by asking him to use a condom, or get into cars with guys who are drunk.

Adapting to the Male World

When girls reach adolescence they move from the safety and intimacy of their female world into the larger world that is male-dominated. Their relational qualities—those characteristics and skills which form the basis of their female identity and which make them feel safe—become discounted by an adult world that stresses self sufficiency, competition, individualism and autonomy. Many girls continue a process of reinventing themselves in order to fit in. As they internalize the values of the male culture, they reject their own and thus lose or diminish a vital part of themselves.

How Girls Deal with Societal Pressures

During adolescence the societal pressures girls experience cause them to split into two selves: the false outward pleasing persona and the real person inside. The more practiced their pleasing persona becomes, the more girls lose their inner voice, their awareness of their own needs and their ability to trust their own perceptions. This causes them to look outward for definition instead of being the center of their own experiences. Girls no longer interact with the world in terms of 'I.' Instead, they relate to it in terms of 'you.' Instead of asking themselves "what do I want" they ask "what do you think of me?"

When girls cannot express their feelings and opinions directly, they do so indirectly by turning against themselves. Girls internalize distress—they draw their pain into themselves. They blame and feel angry with themselves. They learn to speak about themselves in a negative voice. Girls deflect feelings that they cannot express onto their bodies and express them through body dissatisfaction. They tell themselves that they feel fat and ugly and stupid.

Because *fat* is labeled bad in our society, girls encode their feelings in the *language of fat*. Girls 'feel fat' when they are angry, sad, lonely and insecure or when they have no language for their emotions or feel unsafe in expressing themselves. This speaking in code causes girls to shift their focus from their inner experiences of what is real and what

---

STRESSORS IN ADOLESCENCE

↙Societal Pressures↘

↙Media Influences↘

↙Sexism/Racism/Weight Prejudice↘

PHYSICAL CHANGES (Body Issues)	EMOTIONAL CHANGES (Life Issues)
Puberty	Changes in relationships
Increase in Body Fat	Pressure to be kind and nice
Fear of eating/weight gain	Internalization of male values
Self-worth based on appearance	Rejection of female values
Pressure to change body shape	Loss of voice/self-expression
Harassment-objectification	Teasing and bullying
Sexual abuse/violence	Family & life experiences

↘ ↘   ↙ ↙

Disconnection From Body   Disconnection From Self

↘ ↘   ↙ ↙

Internalization Of Distress

↘   ↙

Girls Feel Fat

---

connects them to others to an external self built upon appearance. In so doing, they dissociate from their bodies and from their selves.

Many girls try to alleviate emotional pain or stress in their lives by trying to change their physical bodies. They deal with the discomfort of their real feelings by trying to stop what they see as the source—feeling fat. Dieting provides them with an illusion of control and a temporary sense of achievement. Feeling fat and dieting are the first clear indicators of risk factors that might lead to disordered eating and subsequently to eating disorders.

PUTTING GENDER/DEVELOPMENT KNOWLEDGE INTO PRACTICE

The examples below show how we can apply the framework to real life situations.

Imagine you are having coffee with a small group of women. You are talking about your kids, spouses or mates. One of the men in your office comes in and joins you. Most likely there is an awkward pause as either you change the subject to accommodate him, or he changes the direction in which the conversation is going.

In women-only groups we practice the informal, personal communication style of our female gender culture. Because we have been socialized to fit into the dominant male culture, we automatically adapt ourselves when a man joins our group to his more impersonal cultural pattern of communication instead of asking him to adapt to ours or continuing with own.

Imagine you are having a discussion with a small group of your friends. You are talking about a book or article you have read or a movie you have seen. Everyone is passionate about the subject. The room is alive with energy. Now imagine you have to make a presentation to a large group of people about this very same subject. You begin to translate your ideas into male language and style of communication. In the process you lose your context. This causes you to doubt yourself and your ability. You ask yourself "what do I know?" You are afraid of getting it wrong and doubt yourself even more.

As girls we grow up and play and are therefore comfortable in small groups. When we make presentations or speak to large groups we 'translate' from one gender culture to another. Asking us to speak in larger, more formal groups is similar to asking someone whose first language is English to do a presentation in French. No wonder it is difficult! (In my professional training workshops I have the participants sit together at tables in groups of 8-10 people. Forming connections with their table mates rather than being anonymous within a large group creates safety and makes it easier for them to share their opinions and ideas.)

Kevin is a grade one student. He has difficulty sitting still in class. His writing is messy and he is behind the other students in learning to read. He is becoming really frustrated and is beginning to act out.

Boys develop their fine small motor skills and ability to read and write later than girls. Because they develop their large motor skills earlier they are also more active than girls. Often school is out of sync with their development. Providing Kevin with more physical activity and giving him time to catch up to girls developmentally would help him learn and enable him to feel better about himself.

Peggy is an eighth grade student who is having difficulty with math. When she asks her friends for help, the teacher chastises her for talking. The farther behind she falls, the more inadequate she feels.

Girls are contextual. They learn best when they can personalize the material and relate it to their lives. Providing Peggy with a context for these concepts that is grounded in her experiences and allowing her to work with her friends might make math easier for her and enable her to gain confidence in her ability.

Sources:

Deborah Blum. *Sex on the Brain: The Biological Differences Between Men and Women.* New York: Viking, 1997

Sandra Susan Friedman. *Just for Girls: Facilitator's Manual.* Vancouver: Salal Books, 1999, 2003 (2nd edition)

Sandra Susan Friedman. *When Girls Feel Fat: Helping Girls Through Adolescence.* Toronto: HarperCollins, 1997, 2000 (2nd edition) and Firefly, 2000 (U.S. edition)

Carol Gilligan and Lynn Mikel Brown. *Meeting at the Crossroads: Women's Psychology and Girls' Development.* Cambridge: Harvard University Press, 1992

Michael Gurian. *The Wonder of Boys: What Parents Mentors and Educators Can Do to Shape Boys into Exceptional Men* New York: Jeremy P. Tarcher/Putnam, 1996

Anne Moir and David Jessel. *Brain Sex: The Real Difference between Men and Women.* New York: Bantam Doubleday Dell, 1991

William Pollack. *Real Boys: Rescuing Our Sons from the Myths of Boyhood.* New York: Random House, 1998

Janet L. Surrey. "The Self-in-Relation: A Theory of Women's Development." in Judith Jordan, Alexandra G. Kaplan, Jean Baker Miller, Irene P. Stiver & Janet L. Surrey, eds. *Women's Growth in Connection: Writings from the Stone Center.* New York: Guilford Press, 1991

Catherine M. Shisslak, Marjorie Crago, Linda S. Estes and Norma Gray. "Content and Method of Developmentally Appropriate Prevention Programs." in Linda Smolak, Michael P. Levine and Ruth Streigel-Moore, eds. *The Developmental Psychopathology of Eating Disorders.* New Jersey: Lawrence Erlbaum Associates, 1996

Deborah Tannen. *You Just Don't Understand: Women and Men in Conversatio*n. New York: Ballantine Books, 1990

EATING DISORDERS

Many of us grow up with an uneasy relationship with food and with eating. From an early age we are taught to stop trusting our own bodies and instead put our trust in others who 'know best.' Magazine articles, television, books and even some health professionals tell us there are 'good' foods we should eat but may not want and 'bad' foods we may crave but should not have. We very rarely allow ourselves to have balance but instead focus on foods that we hope will make us lose weight. Dieting for weight loss has become such a normal part of our culture that we continuously alternate not eating enough with eating too much.

Our relationship with food is further complicated by the fact that as women, we are encouraged to prepare food for others but are taught we should not give in to our own appetites and eat. In fact, the way in which we deal with food and eating reflects the tremendous conflict many of us experience around wanting to get our own needs met and our fears that we will be labeled as 'selfish' if we do (a word that is as emotionally loaded as 'fat').

Many of us also grow up with ambivalent feelings about our body shape and size. Regardless of our genetic heritage, we try to conform to a cultural stereotype of an ideal shape that is unhealthy, unrealistic and impossible for most people to achieve. At the present time, we live in a society that has endowed thinness with many magical characteristics such as being sexual, competent, talented, self-confident, intelligent and in control. Imagine choosing a friend or a doctor solely because she is thin. Our preoccupation with thinness has created a societal perception that it is normal for girls and women to experience distress over food, normal to feel discomfort with their body size, normal to strive to eat less and to push themselves to exercise more. It has also resulted in an extreme distaste of fat and an accepted prejudice towards fat people.

It is difficult today for girls to avoid experiencing disordered eating to some degree. Many girls struggle with what to eat, when to eat and how much they should eat. A large number of girls feel fat, and many will become preoccupied with food, weight and body size. While some girls will experiment with eating disorder behaviors, not all girls will develop an eating disorder. Anorexia and bulimia are at the end of a continuum of disordered eating that includes body dissatisfaction, weight preoccupation, chronic 'normalized' dieting, compulsive over-eating, dysfunctional eating and eating disorder practices, including compulsive exercise. Girls with eating disorders are only one or two steps down the continuum from the rest of us.

PROGRESSION OF DISORDERED EATING/ EATING DISORDERS

Healthy body/self image	Girls "feel fat"	Girls become preoccupied with food and weight	Dieting, fasting bingeing, purging exercising	Onset of eating disorders	Medical complications begin	Extreme medical risk

⇒ ⇒

An eating disorder develops when the preoccupation with food and weight escalates to become such an obsession that everything girls do—and all of their feelings—are determined by what they have or haven't eaten that day and by the number on the scale.

Eating disorders are a complex expression of underlying issues with identity and sense of self. They are disorders of human relationships that have been displaced onto the arena of food, appetite and hunger—a response to family dynamics when children are young, to their experiences with their peers, to the environment in which they are raised and to the silencing of their voices in adolescence and the subsequent changes to their relationships. For many girls and women eating disorders are a response to the feelings of powerlessness they experience in their lives. Controlling their body and their food becomes a way of feeling in control of their lives.

Food and Weight Provide the Context for the Behaviors

While eating disorders are expressions of food/weight issues, they are not merely problems with food or with weight, and have very little to do with physiological hunger. Our attitudes towards food and weight and our preoccupation with them do not in themselves create eating disorders but provide the context for them. They are the focus for behaviors that are triggered primarily by psychological need.

Girls are preoccupied with weight and use food to deal with feelings that are too painful or are considered inappropriate to express—such as loneliness, insecurity, anger, fear, sexuality and need. They use them to deal with tension and anxiety, with emotional conflict, and with difficulties for which there don't seem to be any other means of expression or resolution. They use them to hide 'bad' thoughts that don't fit with the societally accepted image of themselves they are trying to create and maintain.

For the compulsive over-eater or binge eater and for the girl with bulimia who does not vomit, food is a way of stuffing down or anesthetizing their feelings. For the girl with bulimia who does vomit, food provides a means to symbolically discharge feelings through purging. For the girl with anorexia, not eating provides symbolic or an illusion of control.

EATING DISORDER BEHAVIORS… externalize the parts of girls
that are deemed *not acceptable* to them or society.

Girls dissociate from those parts of themselves that do not fit the image of a
perfect woman who is thin, passive, independent, unemotional and in control.
They redirect these parts onto their 'fat', their 'bulimia', their 'anorexia'—as though
these were separate entities with lives of their own, containing all the feelings
which are too scary to acknowledge or too difficult to express.

Eating Disorders are Coping Mechanisms

From the moment that we are born each of us has to learn to deal with the world
around us: with our family dynamics, our feelings, our life experiences, the societal
messages and pressures around our gender, and the stressors of everyday life. We learn to
cope by developing indirect ways of dealing with them when it is not safe to address
them directly or when we lack the necessary skills or language, or when we are
overwhelmed by the feelings and stressors in our lives.

Coping mechanisms are thoughts and behaviors we develop and use to manage the
demands that we place upon ourselves and the demands that others place on us that tax or
exceed our individual resources.

Coping has three major functions: 1) *Problem-solving coping* allows us to deal with
the problem that is causing our distress; 2) *Emotion-focused coping* helps us deal with
and regulate the emotions that we experience around the distress and 3) during stressful
periods we attempt to manage and preserve our relationships through *relationship
focused coping*.

Our coping mechanisms vary in intensity depending upon the degree of distress that
we experience. When we examine our coping mechanisms rationally they almost never
make sense. Often they are not even good for us. For example, feeling fat, feeling
worthless, bingeing, purging, starving ourselves and/or exercising excessively may create
psychological and emotional damage and may ultimately make us sick. However, coping
mechanisms serve a valuable function to those people who engage in them. For those
people the alternative is even worse.

Some people may argue that by respecting the coping mechanism we condone the
behaviors and don't provide incentives to change. The reality is that people don't give up
their coping mechanisms until they are ready to do so—until they can replace the
behavior with something else. Instead of reinforcing the shame and guilt girls feel around
their disordered eating behaviors, we need to help them develop the curiosity needed to
find out what's underneath.

EATING DISORDER BEHAVIORS Are Coping Mechanisms Because...

➢ They comfort and nurture girls.

➢ They anesthetize feelings and anxiety.

➢ They are a way of discharging tension, anger and other feelings.

➢ The provide girls with a structure and with an identity.

➢ They are a way of cleansing or purifying the self.

➢ They allow girls to avoid intimacy.

➢ They create a small or large body for protection and/or safety.

➢ They deal with distress by internalizing it.

Adapted from *The Eating Disorder Sourcebook.* Carolyn Costin. Los Angeles: Lowell House, 1996.

DEVELOPING AN EATING DISORDER

Eating disorders develop as a result of the interplay among a combination of factors.

Biology:
➢ Natural weight, height and shape limits.

➢ Predisposition to anxiety or to obsessive-compulsive disorder.

➢ Genetic predisposition such as:

• a relative who has had an eating disorder.

• a short variant of a gene that controls the brain chemical seratonin.. Low seratonin may affect binge eating. High seratonin may affect self- starvation.

Development:
➢ Stage of development affects vulnerability. Girls are most vulnerable during the onset of puberty and then through adolescence.

Socioculture:
➢ Emphasis on appearance as predominant and often only measure of self-worth.

➢ Cultural preoccupation with thinness.

➢ Prejudice and discrimination towards fat people.

➢ Silencing of girls' voices in adolescence.

➢ Devaluation of the female gender culture and pressures to achieve.

Family Dynamics:
➢ Parents who are overly emotional may overwhelm their girls and shut down their feelings, repress their own needs and become the parental caretaker.

➢ Parents who don't have the capacity to tolerate the expression of feelings tend to encourage their girls to close down their feelings.

➢ Parents who use alcohol or drugs make it difficult for girls to connect with them.

➢ Parents who diet, encourage the girl to diet and make comments about weight.

➢ Parents who are overprotective and can't recognize the girl's need for independence.
➢ High family expectation for achievement, looks and/or performance.

Personality Structure and Individual Dynamics:
➢ Perfectionism.
➢ Sense of ineffectiveness, a need to do things right and a fear of doing things wrong.
➢ Loss of relationship.
➢ Lack of boundaries.
➢ Overly concerned with not harming others.

Life Issues:
➢ Ineffective coping mechanisms for daily stressors.
➢ Life events such as loss, trauma, psychological stress.

ANOREXIA NERVOSA

Characteristics

➢ Intense fear of becoming fat regardless of weight loss.
➢ Distorted sense of body weight and shape so that girls may see themselves as fat even when they are emaciated.
➢ Severe dieting and/or fasting.
➢ Significant weight loss (at least 15% of expected body weight).
➢ A perceived need to lose weight even when body weight is very low.
➢ Amenorrhea (loss of menstruation) which raises the risk of osteoporosis.
➢ Fear of food and of situations where food may be present.
➢ Insecurities about abilities regardless of how well she does.
➢ Food rituals such as counting bites of food or cutting food into tiny pieces..
➢ Dizziness and fainting spells.
➢ Complaints of feeling cold.
➢ Withdrawal from people.
➢ Mood swings
➢ Paleness.

Dynamics

Before puberty, slightly more boys than girls develop anorexia nervosa. During and after puberty girls and women are ten times more likely to develop anorexia than boys and men. While the most common age of onset is between 14 and 25 years of age, eating disorders occur in a wide range of ages and are increasingly seen in children as young as ten. Today some women in their late 40s and early 50s are relapsing after overcoming eating disorders in their youth and others are experiencing them for the first time.

Girls (and women) who are anorexic usually begin to diet in response to societal and/or personal stressors. Dieting and weight loss create a sense of well being in them. As people notice them and make positive comments about their weight loss, they feel a tremendous sense of accomplishment. They feel powerful because they know how to lose weight. As they control their food intake girls begin to experience a sense of control in their lives. They don't have to give in to their hunger or eat like other people do. Their feelings of self-worth are determined by what they do not eat. Dieting helps them deal with feelings of meaninglessness, low self-esteem, failure, and dissatisfaction, the need to be unique and the inability to express their anger and their needs. As long as girls deny food they can feel successful, safe and in control.

Often girls who are anorexic use their thinness as a guide to their perceived sense of well-being and self-control. When they feel insecure they poke their ribs to ensure that they are prominent. They check to see if their buttock fits into their hand. They pat their stomach to reassure themselves that it is still flat and even concave. Starving and extreme thinness become necessary for their self-esteem and sense of competence.

Girls with anorexia are preoccupied with food because of physiological hunger, chemical imbalances, psychological dynamics and feelings of deprivation. They prepare food for others, collect recipes and read labels in grocery stores while priding themselves in not giving in. Faced with stress in their lives, they say to themselves: "don't eat." They are afraid if they have one bite, they will lose control and become obese or become overwhelmed by their feelings.

Girls who are anorexic try to fix everything from the outside because they feel they are not good enough inside. Although these girls crave connection they avoid relationships with others because they can't create boundaries. Saying *no* makes them feel selfish and bad. Saying *yes* or taking anything in makes them feel extremely vulnerable and afraid of being overwhelmed. Girls fear rejection and isolation, but even more they fear losing themselves in their attempts to please others. When girls can't create a sense of control or boundaries in their lives the alternate sense of control that seems less threatening to them is controlling their food. Unfortunately this sense of control leads to the eating disorder controlling them.

Girls with anorexia tend to deny or minimize their own needs because they experience dependency and need as weakness and failure. This forces them to try to be self-sufficient and makes it difficult for them to reach out for help. Because of their intense need for approval from others, girls who are anorexic place unrealistic demands on themselves to achieve. They experience criticism as a judgment that they are bad. No matter how well they do, they still feel they have failed. This intensifies feelings of helplessness, lack of control and subsequently their behavior around food.

BULIMIA NERVOSA

Characteristics

- ➢ Regular periods of binge eating and feeling out of control during the eating.
- ➢ Some form of purging in an attempt to prevent weight gain such as self-induced vomiting, abuse of laxatives or diuretics, strict dieting, fasting or excessive exercising.
- ➢ Fear of not being able to stop eating voluntarily.
- ➢ Persistent and driving concern with weight and shape, although the person may be of 'average' weight or 'over' weight or 'under' weight.
- ➢ Depressed mood.
- ➢ Self-deprecating thoughts and shame following eating binges.
- ➢ Secretive eating, sometimes evidenced by missing food.
- ➢ Mood swings that include depression, sadness, guilt and self-hate.
- ➢ Swollen glands, puffiness in the cheeks or broken blood vessels under the eyes.
- ➢ Complains of sore throat, fatigue and/or muscle ache.
- ➢ Unexplained tooth decay.
- ➢ Always goes directly to the bathroom after eating.

Dynamics

Bulimia usually occurs in middle adolescence or young adulthood. Girls who are bulimic restrict their caloric intake in order to maintain a weight that is too low for them and that is dependent upon starvation. Even those girls who are of 'normal' weight or are 'over' weight experience starvation symptoms because they restrict their food intake when they are not bingeing. Although bingeing and purging initially seem like an ideal solution to being able to eat and not gain weight, they soon become entrenched as mood regulators—ways of coping with difficult emotional states. Some girls who are bulimic also use other coping mechanisms like alcohol, drugs and sex.

Girls tend to use food to anesthetize their feelings and to satisfy emotional needs. They deflect feelings that are unacceptable to them onto their fear of gaining weight. They deal with their overwhelming anxiety by purging the food and symbolically purging the feelings as well as the guilt over eating too much food or gaining weight. As the bulimia progresses girls lose the feelings of power and control that they once obtained by defying the effects of overeating. Instead of controlling the bulimia it controls them. Girls constantly think about eating and purging. They structure their day around what they'll eat, when they'll eat and how they will get rid of the calories.

Girls with bulimia have a fragile sense of self and self-worth. Because they look outward to others for definition and approval they are over-pleasing and accommodating.

They hide their anger and their negative feelings from themselves and from others by encoding it in self-deprecation and the language of fat and by disconnecting from themselves and their bodies.

Girls who are bulimic crave closeness and connection. However, because they have difficulty setting limits and boundaries and because of their need to please, their relationships are empty—and they are quick to end them when they become afraid of being taken over by others.

COMPULSIVE OVEREATING
(also called Binge-Eating Disorder)

Characteristics

> ➢ May constantly need to have food nearby.
> ➢ Depressed mood.
> ➢ Feelings of failure, powerlessness and unhappiness.
> ➢ Self-deprecating thoughts following the binges.
> ➢ Restriction of activities because of embarrassment about weight.
> ➢ Feelings about self based on weight and control of eating.
> ➢ Diet related hypertension or fatigue.
> ➢ Cycle of weight loss and weight gain.

Dynamics

People who are compulsive eaters binge eat but do not use extreme compensatory behaviors to lose weight such as fasting or purging. Their bingeing falls into two categories: deprivation-sensitive binge eating results from weight loss diets while addictive or dissociative binge eating comes from using food for self-soothing and as a coping mechanism. As with anorexia and bulimia many people who are compulsive eaters use food to cope with low self-esteem, stress, emotional conflict and powerlessness. Food helps them satisfy their emotional needs and anesthetize their feelings. People who are compulsive eaters have periodic episodes of uncontrolled eating or bingeing. Once the eating is over they feel tremendous guilt and shame and promise themselves that they will never do it again. They go back on the 'diet that will change their life' and over exercise. When deprivation sets in again, they binge, fail the diet and begin the cycle again. This can result in additional weight gain and can also put them at risk of high blood pressure and cardiovascular disease.

Unlike with anorexia and bulimia there is a fairly high proportion of male overeaters. Compulsive eating often runs in families. People struggling with compulsive overeating can be any size or shape. While many often engage in cyclical or yo-yo dieting this does not apply to all people who are fat.

COMPULSIVE EXERCISING

(also called Obligatory Exercise)

Characteristics

➢ Regular episodes of repeatedly exercising beyond what is considered safe.

➢ Addictive behavior.

➢ Emphasis is on weight loss and performance.

➢ Excessive concern about being fat.

➢ Can be a part of anorexia and/or bulimia.

➢ Used as a means of purging and/or reducing anxiety.

➢ Exercise is never for fun.

➢ In athletes, obsessive preoccupation with training. No satisfaction for athletic achievement.

Dynamics

Exercise can place an individual at risk of developing an eating disorder, may serve as a trigger or may coincide with its development. Girls who start out participating in physical activity for fun may begin to use the activity as a way of dealing with stressors in their lives. The more stress they are under, the more compulsive they become around the physical activity. Girls who exercise to burn calories in order to lose weight are at risk of becoming compulsive exercisers. Like dieting, the exercise gives them a sense of temporary power, control and/or self-respect. Like dieting it can soon become obsessive as it becomes a way for girls to deal with underlying issues, with feelings that are difficult to express and with the stressors in their lives.

Girls use exercise as a means of giving themselves permission to eat without gaining weight. Exercise becomes a means for girls to purge or absolve themselves from all of the bad thoughts they have had, the food they have eaten and the situations where they were not perfect. No matter what goes on during the day they will be in control later when their exercise will help them purge themselves of the feelings and punish themselves for their transgressions.

Compulsive exercise is a dangerous way of coping with stress and of avoiding relationships. Most often it is something that girls do alone. Exercising with others makes girls feel out of control because they have to keep up with the other person's pace instead of creating their own. If and when girls are deprived of exercise they feel a tremendous amount of depression, anxiety and guilt.

Because compulsive exercise is addictive it becomes the area of most importance in girls' lives. They will find time to exercise at any cost even if it means skipping school or work, or hiding in the bathroom so that nobody will know what they are doing. Compulsive exercise puts their physical safety, emotional health and other areas of their life such as their school-work and relationships with their families and friends at risk.

Compulsive exercising is becoming a solution to midlife crisis. It is a way for women to avoid looking at what's going on internally and to avoid mourning the things they haven't done in their lives.

Compulsive exercise is harmful. Some of the physical dangers that result are dehydration, stress fracture and degenerative arthritis. Girls and women who over exercise and lose too much body fat will stop menstruating (amenorrea) and become vulnerable to reproductive problems, osteoporosis and heart problems.

Exercise and Athletes

When high school athletes begin training in one particular sport at an elite level they are at greater risk for developing eating disorders than are high school non-athletes. Girls who are ballet dancers, gymnasts, figure skaters, divers and synchronized swimmers have a lot of pressure on them to meet atheistic demands to be thin. Girls who participate in weight lifting, wrestling, martial arts, rowing and sailing must comply with the weight classifications of their sport. Girls who participate in distance running, cycling, triathlon, swimming and cross country skiing are told that being thin enhances their performance. And what can we say about sports such as beach volleyball where media and sports federations emphasize sexuality more than athleticism.

Athletes who have a desire to succeed often succumb to the misconception that weight loss and excessive training improve performance. Not only are they bombarded with these messages by coaches but also by parents who want them to succeed and peers who have internalized and thus reinforce these messages. Girls who want to satisfy the expectations of others and perform well learn to measure their self worth by their body size and their looks. Once they get caught up in performance and looks they are unable to enjoy their abilities or see them as one dimension of their lives. They make exercise their entire life. They focus on nothing but their sport, their training schedules and their injuries. Even when injured, they will not take time off.

One of the greatest risks and most serious health concerns for athletes is the Female Athlete Triad which includes eating disorders, amenorrhea— when an athlete misses her menstrual period for three months or hasn't started menstruating by age sixteen, and osteoporosis— where the bones lose their density and become weak, brittle and fragile making girls more prone to fractures.

EATING DISORDERS IN MALES

About 10 to 15% of people with eating disorders are male. Of these 4 to 6% have anorexia, 10 to 13% have bulimia and 79 to 83% are compulsive eaters. While some boys develop anorexia before puberty, males tend to develop eating disorders between the ages of 18 and 26 years old.[1]

In the past few years preoccupation with and importance of appearance for men has dramatically increased. In a 1997 *Psychology Today* survey of 548 men, 43% reported they were dissatisfied with their appearance, 17% said they would give up more than three years of their lives to be able to reach their weight goals and 11% said they would sacrifice 5 years.

From the time boys are young they receive messages normalizing an exaggerated body size that is impossible to attain—beginning with toys such as G.I. Joe and Star Wars action figures. In the last 20 years the ideal male presented in the *Playgirl* centerfolds has lost about 12 pounds of fat while putting on approximately 27 pounds of muscle. Magazines, fashion, hair and cosmetic industries have developed that are devoted to making men "look good' which means trim and buff. Eighty-four percent of men believe that physical attractiveness is important to succeed, 48% of men belong to health clubs Cosmetic surgery is on the rise. Boys and men internalize those messages and hold themselves to unrealistic standards. As they try to change their bodies many get caught up in the psychological dynamics of dieting and exercise.

Males with eating disorders often have issues that are similar to those of girls and women. These include perfectionist attitudes, family backgrounds that include rigid rules and high expectations, genetic disposition, parents who are preoccupied with weight, low self-esteem, and lack of autonomy. Many men suffer from depression and have difficulty coping with emotions or personal issues in their lives. During adolescence boys who are homosexual may use disordered eating as a way of dealing with conflicts around their sexual orientation and society's attitudes towards their sexuality.

Boys and men who are at high risk of developing eating disorders may have a history of obesity or of being 'over' weight. They begin dieting as a response to teasing by their peers and to the shame that they feel. Males who participate in sports where there is a required weight and where weight is monitored and/or who strive for increased performance through weight loss or exercise are at greater risk of developing an eating disorder as are males who diet as a way of dealing with weight gain when they have a sports injury. Men who are in the entertainment industry seem to be at higher risk for developing an eating disorder because of the added pressure on body image/appearance.

---

[1] Boston College Eating Awareness Team. January 28, 2002

Men who lose weight in order to avoid weight-related illnesses that run in their families can sometimes take weight loss too far. It can be hard to detect boys and men with eating disorders because they must deal with the stigma of having what is seen to be a woman's disease. Men will struggle with eating disorders for years before they will get help. They are less likely to place themselves into a situation that involves acknowledging and dealing with feelings.

MUSCLE DYSMORPHIA
(also called Bigarexia)

Characteristics

- Distorted sense of body shape.
- Irrational fear of being too small or not muscular.
- Frequently measures body (biceps, chest, waist).
- Chooses clothes that make him look more muscular or wears several layers of clothes to look bigger.
- Spends large amounts of money on special foods and dietary supplements.
- Regular episodes of repeatedly working out beyond the requirements of what is considered safe.
- Is addictive behavior.
- Uses steroids.

Dynamics

Images of men today reflect more male muscle and rippled chests than ever before. The ideal man with his hard and muscular body physically reinforces society's tough, hard and unemotional code of masculinity. Because thinness is usually equated with weakness and frailty, boys and men who have body image concerns or feel powerless in their lives want to bulk up instead of lose weight. Some take bigness to an extreme.

Muscle dysmorphia is often called bigarexia or 'reverse anorexia' because the individual thinks he cannot get big enough or muscular enough. While it affects some women, it is more prevalent in men who see parts of their body as being too scrawny. In an effort to 'fix' their perceived smallness, they engage in resistance or weight training and exercise beyond what is considered healthy and safe.

Men with muscle dysmorphia work out compulsively. They repeatedly check themselves in mirrors and feel deeply depressed after missing even one day of weight lifting. Because weight training and exercise become addictive they slowly take over the individual's time and life. Men take steroids to build bigger muscles and even then they aren't satisfied with how they look.

Steroid use is on the rise today and the age at which they are being used is getting lower. While pressure from coaches and sports teams contribute to steroid use as do gyms that make steroids available not all steroid use is related to sports. Teenage boys and young men may try anabolic steroids (synthetic versions of the hormone testosterone) in an attempt to gain control of their lives by controlling their bodies. As appearance becomes more and more a measure of self-worth boys and young men try to conform to the societal ideal. Ten year old boys and high school students who do not play sports bulk up with steroid precursors simply because they want to look good—especially to girls.

Steroids and steroid precursors such as androstenedione (which was used by baseball player Mark McGuire) increase muscle size and help increase strength by giving muscles the potential to grow bigger and stronger more quickly. However, their side effects can stifle bone growth and can include increased aggression and mood swings, damage to the liver and kidneys, testicular shrinkage, balding, acne, high blood pressure and increased cholesterol levels which may lead to heart disease. Taking steroids by injection increases the risk of contracting hepatitis B and C and HIV, the virus that causes AIDS.

Sources:

Arnold Anderson, MD, Leigh Cohn, MAT & Thomas Holbrook, MD. *Making Weight: Men's Conflicts with Food, Weight, Shape and Appearance.* Carlsbad, CA: Gurze Books, 2000

Anorexia Nervosa and Related Eating Disorders, Inc. (ANRED)   http://www.anred.com

Ginia Bellafante. "When Midlife Seems Just an Empty Plate." *NY Times*, March 9, 2003

Boston College Eating Awareness Team   www.bc.edu/bc_org

School Outreach Program Training Manual. British Columbia Eating Disorders Association, November, 1988

Catrina Brown & Karin Jasper. "The Continuum of Anorexia, Bulimia and Weight Preoccupation," in Catrina Brown & Karin Jasper, eds. *Consuming Passions: Feminist Approaches to Weight Preoccupation and Eating Disorders.* Toronto: Second Story Press, 1993

Carolyn J. Cavanaugh, and Ray Lemberg. "What we know about eating disorders: facts and statistics," in Raymond Lemberg and Leigh Cohn, eds. *Eating Disorders: A reference sourcebook.* Phoenix, AZ: Oryx Press, 1999

Carolyn Costin. *The Eating Disorder Sourcebook: A Comprehensive Guide to the Causes, Treatments and Prevention of Eating Disorders.* Los Angeles: Lowell House, 1996, 1997

Timothy Eagan. "Body Conscious Boys Adopt Athletes' Taste for Steriods," *NY Times*, November 22, 2002

"Do I have an eating disorder?" Eating Disorder Resource Centre of British Columbia flyer

Sandra Susan Friedman. *Just for Girls.* Vancouver, BC: Salal Books, 1999, 2003 (2nd edition)

Sandra Susan Friedman. *When Girls Feel Fat: Helping Girls Through Adolescence.* Toronto: HarperCollins, 1997, 2000 (2nd edition) and Firefly, 2000 (US edition)

Something Fishy Website on Eating Disorders   www.something-fishy.org

Harrison G. Pope, JR., MD, Katharine A. Phillips, MD, and Roberto Olivardia, MD. *The Adonis Complex: The Secret Crisis of Male Body Obsession.* Free Press, 2000

Drugs and Sport: The Score. Royal Canadian Mounted Police Drug Awareness Program

Michele Siegel, Ph.D., Judith Brisman, Ph.D., & Margot Weinshel, M.S.W. *Surviving An Eating Disorder: Strategies for Family and Friends.* New York: HarperPerennial, 1988

PREVENTION

Prevention of eating disorders (what is often called *primary* prevention) takes place 'before the fact.' It occurs right at the beginning of the progression of disordered eating at the point where girls still feel good about their bodies and themselves, and just before they begin to feel fat or diet or experiment with other forms of weight control behavior. Prevention is not about eating disorders per se; it is about promoting and sustaining healthy development—including developing healthy coping strategies, positive self-esteem, body image, identity and celebrating diversity in body size and shape.

Eating disorder prevention also addresses obesity. Although genetic factors and physiology play a role in the development both of eating disorders and of children being fat, the dramatic increases we are seeing are also a result of environmental and social factors. These factors can be addressed using the skills and strategies and developmental framework presented in this book. By addressing the entire spectrum of weight issues we can end the conflicting messages girls receive about their relationship to food, weight and body size. Above all, prevention is about nurturing *girlpower,* and likewise preventing the disengagement of boys.

Girls with *girlpower*

> ➤ Can express their feelings constructively.
> ➤ Are able to set boundaries.
> ➤ Have healthy connections with others.
> ➤ Develop their self-esteem in areas other than looking good.
> ➤ Have a good sense of their bodies.
> ➤ Are physically active.
> ➤ Have a healthy relationship with food.

Prevention is Like a Pizza

It helps to see prevention as a pizza: The crust is made up of gender, development and the impact of society on girls and boys. The base (tomato sauce) consists of the developmental / life stages. Each topping represents a different social or health risk and the factors and conditions that are particular to it. While some risk factors such as dieting are particular to eating disorders and obesity, others such as the silencing of girls' voices are also present in other behaviors or conditions. As a result, the same prevention strategies that address eating disorder prevention can also be used or adapted to address smoking, sexually transmitted diseases (STDs), alcohol and drugs, teen pregnancy and depression.

Prevention Addresses Different Stages of Development

Prevention begins with **pre-** and **postnatal women** and continues through the different life stages. During middle adolescence prevention overlaps with early intervention as girls may begin to experiment with eating disorder behaviors.

Girls and boys become vulnerable to the risk of eating disorders even before they are born. While their mothers may welcome their pregnancies, they may also feel out of control as their bodies begin to expand. Once the baby is born many women find it very difficult to cope with the demands made upon them, often at the expense of their own needs. Because of societal myths surrounding motherhood such as self-sacrifice and unconditional love many women feel guilty for sometimes wishing that babies were refundable—at least for short periods of time. Like adolescent girls, women who are unable to directly express their feelings about their lives deflect them onto their bodies and encode them in a language of fat. Many women deal with the stressors in their lives after the birth of a baby by becoming preoccupied with their weight and body shape. They feel fat and diet in an attempt to gain control of their lives. They measure themselves according to how they look and may transmit these attitudes and behaviors onto their child.

In **early childhood** feeding problems as well as food restriction may lead to other problems later on. As girls and boys grow up, they move through different stages of physical, emotional and cognitive development. In each stage of development their life experiences and the relationship they have with their families play a large role in how they interact with the world. The risk to **children** of developing unhealthy coping mechanisms is magnified in families where there is an absence of boundaries or where the boundaries are too rigid, where there is divorce, a recent death of family members or pets, birth of siblings, constant conflict, step-parents (and blended families), parental mental illness, use of alcohol and/or drugs and/or the chronic illness of a family member. Unhealthy coping mechanisms also develop in situations where there is sexual abuse, sexism, the experience of or witness to violence, and obsessive emphasis on weight and shape.

Preadolescent girls must deal with the beginnings of the social, emotional and physical changes that occur during puberty. Girls' bodies vary widely because of genetic and biological factors—yet they are all expected to look the same. A predisposition to perfectionism, as well as low self-esteem, and teasing and bullying about being fat all become risk factors as do the changing dynamics of friendship. As girls begin to withhold their feelings and opinions they become vulnerable to the dark side of friendship that includes secrets and exclusion. Shunning is a painful form of bullying peer groups enforce. Often the one being shunned isn't even aware of the reason.

In **early adolescence** (girls are between the ages of 11 and 13), the issues that have the greatest impact on girls arise from the changes in their bodies and the changes in their lives. Girls who are early bloomers are at greater risk because they mature earlier and therefore accumulate fat. Girls who develop later may perceive their bodies as abnormal. Some girls find the transition from the safety of their elementary or middle school to a large, impersonal high school to be difficult. Although they may make new friends, they also lose old friends and must deal with general insecurity around friendships. Girls start becoming interested in romantic relationships at this stage of development. They also experience problems with their parents as they attempt to become more autonomous. They begin to lose their aerobic capacity as they avoid physical education classes and stop using their bodies.

In the **middle stages of adolescence** (around 14 to 16 years old), girls deal with balancing their need for maintaining connection with their families and their need for increasing independence. Girls this age need to deal with romantic relationships and with sexuality. They feel anxiety, loss and self-doubt over losing friendships that are often tenuous at best. They experience more pressure to achieve better grades in school and pressure from the media to be perfect and confident. They internalize the societal construct that this means being *thin*.

In **later adolescence** (around 17 to 19 years old) girls must deal with the transition from high school to college or to the workplace and possibly with leaving home. Some girls internalize male values and place most of their self-esteem on achievement at school or at work at the expense of their relationships. Girls need to deal with the stressors of daily life. They need to deal with creating a balance between old ties and new relationships, with sexuality and with balancing their needs with the needs and wants of others. They need to counteract unrelenting messages from the media that they should be thin, perfect, confident and in control.

Some **women in their late 40's and early 50's** relapse after overcoming eating disorders when they were younger while others are experiencing them for the first time. Many of these women spend their days around hours of jogging, tennis and other calorie-burning activities. They use compulsive exercise and other eating disorder behaviors to deal with (or avoid dealing with) the anxieties of midlife — divorce, marital strains, parental deaths, empty-nest syndrome and menopause. When women base their self-esteem on how they look and repress their feelings they become more vulnerable to the fear of aging which is a powerful catalyst in a culture that for the past 20 years has been obsessed with fitness, thinness and on looking 23 when you are 45.

Prevention is both Universal and Selective

Prevention is both universal and selective. That is, universally it should be targeted towards all girls and boys in a variety of settings throughout development. Before puberty prevention efforts should be directed at girls and boys who have not yet internalized the slender ideal. Boys and girls can be together in situations where we want them to learn from and about each other and where we are providing information that both can benefit from—as long as it is not about a vulnerable area in their lives.

Along with universal prevention, additional selective prevention efforts should specifically target girls throughout the developmental challenges of puberty and adolescence because they are at increased risk for negative body image and disordered eating. These prevention efforts should take place in same sex groups or classes. If we want to prevent the silencing of girls' voices, encourage them to share their feelings, voice their opinions, validate each other and build and nurture their relationships and female culture and if we want to teach skills, then we need to separate the girls from the boys. Adolescent girls are developmentally and socially more mature than boys their own age. They also want these potential boyfriends to like them. Having even one boy present changes the group dynamics as the girls stop sharing their real concerns and start focusing on the boy.

Because boys are increasingly developing body image concerns that may result in body image dissatisfaction, disordered eating, steroid use and muscle dysmorphic disorder, specific programs and strategies need to directly address their concerns. These programs and strategies should be implemented in all-male settings. They should be adapted to and made appropriate for the male gender culture. They should also be implemented by men.

Prevention Identifies and Addresses Risk Factors

A risk factor is something that makes a person vulnerable to developing a specific problem and occurs before the problem develops. The greatest risk factors in developing an eating disorder are dieting, social comparison, body dissatisfaction— which often results when girls project the feelings and thoughts that they cannot express onto their bodies—and dieting and teasing. Internalizing the values and behaviors of the male culture and rejecting their own female ones is also a big risk factor for girls.

Psychologist Catherine Steiner-Adair explored the conflicts between the relational aspects of female identity and the societal image of independence, achievement and autonomy. Two distinct patterns emerged. 'Wise women' recognized societal pressure for achievement and independence, but were able to acknowledge and value the importance of relationships. They were at less risk for eating disorders. 'Superwomen' identified with an ideal woman who was successful in different roles that gained her external approval and who saw the ideal woman as independent, tall and thin, and not needing anyone else. They were at much greater risk of developing an eating disorder because their strong identification with societal values were in conflict with and often replaced their developmental needs for connection.

RISK FACTORS

➢ Body Dissatisfaction — ranging from disliking entire body and size to focusing on a specific body part.

➢ Social comparison.

➢ Teasing.

➢ Dieting.

➢ Loss of voice or ability to express feelings and opinions.

➢ Changes in relationships.

➢ Internalization of male values and ideals.

➢ Low self-esteem.

➢ Peer groups where there is a high concern about weight.

➢ Parents who model and stress the importance of thinness.

➢ Media and high exposure to unhealthy and unrealistically thin body image ideals.

➢ Specific high risk activities such as participation in ballet or in sports where there is a weight category or that emphasize thinness and body shape.

➢ Physical activity which stresses or is based on weight loss.

➢ Being fat.

Prevention Sets in Place Protective Factors Through K.I.S.S.

Prevention attempts to set in place protective factors in order to decrease the likelihood eating disorders will develop. I have named the progression prevention strategies and programs should follow *K.I.S.S*—which refers to *Knowledge, Interaction/ Action, Skills* and *Support*.

Knowledge

The first step in prevention is providing *Knowledge* or giving information. Dr. Susan J. Paxton, a psychologist with the University of Melbourne reviewed the existing research literature for body image/eating disorder prevention programs. She found that many programs are knowledge based. While some are limited to one session such as classroom presentations, the majority or programs offer 5 to 10 classroom sessions. These sessions usually address body image and eating issues in an attempt to reduce the internalization of the thin ideal for girls, the excessively muscular ideal for boys and the importance placed on thinness by providing more realistic information. They also aim to provide information that might prevent girls from developing disordered eating behaviors as a consequence of 'normal' dieting.

Girls (and boys) need to know about the changes in their bodies during puberty so that they will not feel that they or their weight gain is abnormal. Learning about genes and metabolism provide an understanding about why people are different sizes and shapes and helps decrease fat prejudice. Knowing what happens when people diet and use steroids and what different foods do to their bodies helps girls and boys make healthy choices. They also need to be able to realistically analyze the messages of the media so that they don't internalize them or blindly respond to them.

When we provide girls and boys with *Knowledge*, we need to make sure that instead of just talking at them we include a dialogue with them. We need to give them time to think about the information and process it. We also need to provide them with the opportunity to come back and clarify what they don't understand.

While knowledge is important, it cannot be the only prevention strategy. Programs that increase knowledge and awareness widen a person's view of herself or himself and her or his environment in a manner that may later be psychologically protective. However, they do not translate into changed attitudes, beliefs and behaviors.

Interaction/Action

Interaction/Action is the second step of prevention. Programs that include strongly interactive and participatory components seem more successful than those that are didactic. We can provide *Interaction/Action* opportunities through experiential activities such as movement, drawing, role plays, problem solving and small group discussion depending on the setting. Written activities such as handouts are a good way to raise awareness, stimulate discussion, give girls quiet times to think about themselves and provide a lead-in to specific activities. When we use handouts we need to remind girls they cannot fail and remind ourselves handouts do not replace discussion about and validation of their real life experiences. If we are teachers we need to stop ourselves from getting carried away and grading them.

We need to ensure *Interaction/Action* takes place in the context of girls' lives and provide them with a context for their behaviors. For example, you can't teach healthy eating without addressing why girls are afraid to eat or self esteem without looking at how girls feel powerless or accepting your body and the pressures to be thin.

Skills

The third and most important part of prevention is teaching *Skills* so that girls can deal with the stressors in their lives in a healthy way. For example, giving girls information about why dieting is harmful and discussing what happens when you diet and the pressures to diet provide *Knowledge*. Charting dieting history is a good *Interaction/Action*. However, if you want to prevent girls from beginning to diet or to get them to stop dieting then you need to teach them *Skills* to deal with teasing, peer pressure and feeling fat—all factors that contribute to why they begin to diet in the first place.

Support

If we are going to teach girls new behaviors and encourage them to practice a way of being in the world that is different from what they are told by the media and society, then we must also be there to give them support. This means validating them and encouraging them when they try out the new behavior, providing ongoing prevention strategies and programs that support them through different stages of development and life transitions, modeling the same behaviors we are teaching them and advocating for them when they challenge traditional ways for girls to be in the world. In supporting girls we can provide them with a solid foundation for their beliefs and behaviors so they can feel safe in exercising their *girlpower* and in being true to themselves.

Prevention Addresses Changes in Girls Bodies *and* in their Lives

Prevention equally addresses the changes that take place in girls' bodies *and* in their lives during adolescence. The tendency of many prevention programs is to focus just on body image, the pressure to be thin, healthy eating, the hazards of dieting and on promoting physical activity. When we don't address the silencing of girls' voices we run the risk of silencing them in the same way the culture does, and inadvertently reinforce the very dynamics that we say we are trying to change. On the other hand, if we only address the silencing of girls' voices and their loss of self-esteem, then we leave them without the skills to accept, value and enjoy their bodies and normalize their eating and without the resources to fight back against societal pressure to disconnect from their bodies and define themselves solely in terms of how they look.

BODY ISSUES

The Grungies—this is a term coined to describe your negative voice. Every time you tell yourself that you feel fat or are fat, ugly or stupid you have been "hit by a grungie." Underneath every grungie there is a real story waiting to be told.

Puberty Education—teaches girls about the changes in their bodies. We need to provide them with a safe place to ask the questions that are of real concern to them.

MAJOR COMPONENTS OF PREVENTION

BODY ISSUES:	LIFE ISSUES:

Dealing with the *grungies*

Puberty education	Understanding gender culture
Metabolism/Genetics	Building healthy relationships
Eating for energy/strength	Encouraging self-expression
Body awareness/appreciation	Media literacy/activism
Enouraging physical activity	Fighting the power of appearance
Size acceptance	Ending teasing/bullying

Metabolism and Genetics—let girls understand why they have the body that they do. Understanding why people have different body types and sizes helps normalize fat and break down the prejudices around it.

Eating for Energy and Strength—teaches girls about balance and what foods do and helps normalize food and resolve the uneasy relationship that girls develop around it.

Body Awareness and Appreciation—helps girls develop an internal and kinesthetic sense of their bodies so they can redirect their focus to how they feel inside.

Physical Activity—encourages girls to use their bodies to develop physical strength, flexibility and self-confidence and to remain connected to their bodies.

Encouraging Size Acceptance—values girls of all shapes and sizes and fights fat prejudice.

LIFE/SELF ISSUES

Validating Gender Culture—helps girls understand why they travel in pairs, why their friendships are so important and why it is sometimes so difficult to talk to boys.

Encouraging Self-Expression—helps girls maintain their voice or confidence in their ideas, perceptions and feelings.

Building Healthy Relationships—helps girls develop limits and boundaries, understand what draws them to people and what makes them move away. It teaches girls communication skills and conflict resolution skills.

Media Literacy/ Activism —teaches girls how to critically evaluate and break down media images and how to challenge and change unrealistic standards.

Fighting the Power of Appearance—helps girls develop self esteem, identify and develop skills and qualities other than looking good.

Addressing Bullying—makes schools and other environments safer for girls.

Prevention is Both Integrated and Program-Based

In order for prevention to be successful it needs to be ongoing so it can reinforce skills, change beliefs and attitudes towards food, weight and body shape and support girls and boys through developmental transitions. While most of us don't have the time, mandate and resources to address every element of prevention, we can integrate basic elements into our individual practice and into our school curricula and community programs. The *basic elements* listed below are the ones I consider the most important and are addressed in more detail further on in this book.

Basic Elements of Prevention:

> Teaching girls about the grungies

> Countering the power of appearance

> Promoting size acceptance

Once we have addressed the basic elements of prevention we can supplement and complement them with prevention programs that address specific components in greater detail and can be targeted at girls and boys who are at risk. Because programs are usually time limited they should not be the only form of prevention.

Sources:

Catherine Steiner-Adair. "The Body Politic: Normal Female Adolescent Development and the Development of Eating Disorders." *Journal of the American Academy of Psychoanalysis*, 55, 567- 576, 1986

Susan J. Paxton. "Research Review of Body Image Programs: An Overview of Body Image Dissatisfaction Prevention Interventions." Department of Human Services, Melbourne, Victoria, Australia, July 2002

Catherine M. Shisslak, Marjorie Crago, Linda S. Estes & Norma Gray. "Content and Method of Developmentally Appropriate Prevention Programs." in Linda Smolak, Michael P. Levine & Ruth Streigel-Moore, eds. *The Developmental Psychopathology of Eating Disorders*. New Jersey: Lawrence Erlbaum Associates, 1996

IMPLEMENTING PREVENTION STRATEGIES

No one person or group, program or organization can be responsible for all of prevention because eating disorders are multi-faceted. A comprehensive approach requires the participation of individuals, the immediate social environment such as the family and the school, and the wider community. Everyone can integrate the basic elements of prevention into their practice while specific issues or components can be addressed through prevention programs. Some of the components that are described on the previous pages can be integrated into the school or are a part of the school curriculum. Some are addressed in other prevention programs, through community organizations, youth groups, parks and recreation and fitness centers. Currently, organizations within the field of eating disorders and obesity prevention are working together to provide common messages that promote health and well being.

A Comprehensive Approach Includes:

➤ Educating teachers, staff, parents and students and community organizations about gender and development, the risks girls and boys are vulnerable to and prevention strategies that they can implement.

➤ Ensuring that everyone addresses the basic elements so that messages can be consistent and skills can be reinforced.

➤ Creating a body-friendly environment in the school, home and community that values people of all shapes and sizes and all races and cultures.

➤ Working with families, schools and the community to promote healthy eating and food choices.

➤ Encouraging families, schools and the community to promote physical activity.

➤ Working with schools to end teasing and bullying.

ADDRESSING PREVENTION INDIVIDUALLY

Many of us are involved with eating disorder prevention through our individual efforts. We integrate the basic elements into our practice. We facilitate groups, do presentations, address prevention in our classrooms or with community groups or with individual girls whom we are involved with. Some of us implement very specific programs and/or resources. Regardless of our level of understanding and experience with eating disorder prevention we each bring with us skills and competence in our lives and our work we can apply to prevention and to working with girls.

The participants in the professional training workshops that I facilitate are often a mix of public health nurses, community nurses, school nurses and psychiatric nurses, nutritionists, dietitians, school counselors, alcohol and drug counselors, women's center workers and private practitioners, childcare workers, teachers, fitness and dance instructors, university students and parents. Sometimes workshops include high school girls. No matter how much experience they have, a strange phenomenon seems to occur as the women arrive at the session: women who are wonderfully competent in many other aspects of their lives begin discounting their skills and experiences and placing a lot of pressure on themselves to be 'experts'. Many of them say things like: "Oh, if I only had a PhD, if I only had four more courses, if I only had more experience, then I would be able to do this." As the introductions begin, the women compare themselves to each speaker. "This woman is more articulate," they tell themselves, "This woman has more experience." In making these comparisons they put themselves down.

Like the girls we work with we too tend to look outside of ourselves for definition and direction and in the process discount our skills and ourselves. In prevention we look to 'experts' for the 'best' practice or perfect strategy or resource. When we find we cannot relate personally to some resource or strategy, we don't question its appropriateness or wonder how girls will relate to it if we can't, but question instead our ability to apply it. Yet, we need to be able to relate personally to eating disorder skills, strategies and programs. They need to make sense to us before we can implement them into our work. Instead of discounting ourselves, we need to name and value our skills regardless of how familiar—and therefore unimportant—they may seem to us. This enables us to transfer our skills from one area of expertise to another, instead of constantly feeling we need to reinvent the wheel.

As you work through this manual remember two things: you cannot fail eating disorder prevention, and there is no one specific way of doing it right. We all bring with us certain skills and talents. We all have some ability to relate to others. We enter into the training process and practice at our own particular level of experience and interest. We need to respect who we are. When we get caught up in performance anxiety, we lose our curiosity—the main ingredient we need in order to learn.

You and I may implement the very same strategies and teach the very same skills, but do it differently because we are different people. In my professional training workshops the most valuable learning often takes place between the women themselves as they share their experiences. So does the recognition that nutritionists may practice differently from teachers, who may practice differently from women's center workers or youth workers and so forth. Not only would their practice be different, so would the subject matter that would be their focus. Once you too can understand you are not responsible for all of prevention—and everything you can contribute is valuable, you can take the focus off 'experts' and bring it back to yourself where it belongs.

Schmoozing — Sharing Yourself with Girls

Prevention is about promoting and sustaining healthy development —helping girls deal with the changes in their bodies and in their lives and with the challenges of adolescence. It makes sense, then, the most essential ingredients we bring to prevention are our own experiences of growing up female and the gender dynamics and characteristics we have in common with girls. Our four PhDs or ten more post-graduate courses are not half as important as our willingness to model healthy female relationships by engaging honestly with girls, by letting them know what we think and what we feel, and by sharing our own experiences of the world with girls instead of trying to tell them what to do.

One of the most powerful ways for us to share ourselves with girls is to *schmooze* with them. *Schmoozing* is a Yiddish word that means talking informally or 'chewing the fat.' I use the term *schmoozing* to describe the communication ritual we use with each other, especially when sharing our problems.

When I have a problem, for example, I telephone a friend and say something like: "Oh, I can't believe what just happened! I really need to talk!" When I put the problem into words it makes it real. This is important because many of us tend to minimize our experiences. My friend might say: "Ooh, that's terrible, that's really difficult, I can't believe it, you must be so upset!" Her empathic response validates my feelings and lets me know I have a right to the way I feel. This is important because we often tend to worry about the other person's feelings instead of our own. My friend then shares a similar problem of her own, saying "Oh, the same thing happened to me!" If she doesn't have a similar problem, she shares someone else's. Knowing other people have similar experiences reassures me I am normal and helps me feel less isolated. After we have schmoozed for a while she might give me feedback or brainstorm strategies with me. When I hang up the phone, the problem might still be there, but schmoozing (expressing it and taking it seriously and having it validated and normalized) makes me feel better about myself and helps me take myself seriously which makes the problem easier to resolve.

SCHMOOZING

Talking about our problem makes it real...
...because we tend to discount our experiences

Empathy from others lets us know we have a right to the way we feel...
...because we tend to negate our feelings or focus on how the other person felt instead of on ourselves.

The sharing of a similar problem lets us know we are not alone in how we feel...
...because we think we are abnormal and the only one who feels the way we do.

As adults, we schmooze mainly with other adults. We rarely schmooze with girls. One of the reasons is we have been taught to see prevention as providing information and warnings such as "don't diet," "don't have sex," don't hang out with your friends." We have been taught if we tell girls what to do and give them a logical rationale for doing it, they will listen to us and change their behavior. However, when we *talk at* girls instead of *listening to* them, girls distance themselves from us and tune us out.

Helping girls deal with body issues and developmental/life stage issues requires that we adults bring our personal selves into our professional lives. Girls are more willing to communicate when we share ourselves with them. This does not mean we tell them about our messy divorce or use them as a sounding board for issues that we are in the process of working out. It means we selectively share similar experiences of ours as a way of normalizing theirs, of giving them permission to raise certain topics, and of giving them language to help them when they have trouble describing what they feel. By sharing our experiences with girls we validate theirs and form a connection with them that facilitates their growth.

Sharing ourselves with girls can be difficult for those of us who have been trained to view our professionalism as based on hierarchy and on keeping distance from our client. Remembering our own adolescence can be painful for some of us because it brings up memories that we consider best left forgotten. Often we don't share our experiences with girls because we are afraid to 'burden' them. We think if we don't talk to girls about the guys who dumped us or we don't share our own moments of insecurity and doubt we will spare them that pain. By not talking with girls about our experiences, we rob them of a context for their own experiences. Instead of giving them support, we set them adrift.

When girls begin to articulate the stories that arise out of discussions about their body issues or that are underneath their *grungies* (negative voice), we find the issues they are dealing with are the same, or very similar, to those we constantly deal with as grown women. Girls talk about relationships and their difficulties in being true to themselves while not hurting anyone else. They talk about the pain of rejection and how hard it is to be regarded as different. They talk about sexuality and harassment and their ambivalent feelings about their changing bodies. They talk about taking care of others and not getting their own needs met. And while we want to validate their experiences by sharing our own, it's not easy when the issues girls raise are the ones that are so emotionally charged for us, or when their value system or means of coping are very different from ours.

As women who work with girls we must constantly try to understand what life looks like for girls—to continuously ask them about their feelings and what their experiences mean to them in the context of their lives. We need to monitor ourselves for commonalties where we can relate to the girls. When we don't relate to their experiences we still need to find a way to validate them without judging them or minimizing their feelings or feeling the need to 'fix' their lives.

Working with girls makes us take stock of our *shoulds*. We *should:* always be right, know the answer, agree with other people, be patient, share when we don't want to, never get angry, never say no. When we turn off our heads and open our hearts, we know when we feel connected to someone else and when we feel safe, heard, understood and accepted—regardless of whether they agree with us or not. When that connection is broken, we feel abandoned, judged, wronged and criticized.

Girls respond when they feel an emotional bond with women who are honest about their feelings and opinions. We don't always have to know the answer, or be patient, or agree with their behavior or points of view—as long as we are honest in our interactions with them. We lose them the moment we cease to be ourselves. When we assume our formal and authoritative adult voices, we become part of the dominant culture. When we give girls information or practice exercises that are not set in the context of their lives and experiences, the girls close down. Many feel unsafe because of the dissonance between what they are being taught and what they experience inside.

Empowering girlpower

When we teach girls the skills that help them remain connected to their selves, we introduce them to an image of women and girls that it is different from those prevailing in our society. We offer them dynamic choices and encourage self-expression in place of the mantle of passivity and self-repression they are expected to assume as they grow up. However, in encouraging girls to be assertive and in steering them back to their own culture, we may put them at risk of disapproval and adverse reaction from their parents, their teachers and their friends. We need to be there to support girls by letting them know they have a right to how they feel and by teaching them communication skills that will allow them to express themselves in a way that lets them be heard. We need to teach them how to deal with their hurt and disappointment and the hurts and disappointments of others. We need to model the same behavior we are teaching girls and be willing advocates for them as they require.

Acknowledging Our Own Weight Prejudice

As women we are also products of the culture in which girls mature and are influenced by these same pressures. We need to be able to acknowledge our own weight prejudice and monitor our language and actions for signs of it. Despite our best intentions, we pass our attitudes along to the girls. The girls in one school talked about a well-meaning teacher who brought cookies in for the class. Realizing there were not enough to go around, the teacher said: "Only the thin kids will get cookies. The fat kids don't need them."

When we work with girls we must be able to accept a range of body types and sizes. This means that we do not fall prey to the myth that equates being fat with being unhealthy or undisciplined, or the myth that everyone wants to be thin—and can be if they try hard enough.

We need to value our bodies as functional and beautiful, no matter what size they are. We must recognize that you can be fat and healthy if you are active and that diets don't work, regardless of the circumstances. We must also be able to value people for who they are and what they have to offer. Because we are constantly bombarded by the same messages from the media as the girls, we must consciously question and negate and refute what those images of perfection are and what they mean.

Most of us struggle to varying degrees with our natural bodies. If you see fat as bad, if you are presently dieting, if you have a strong belief that losing weight and eating only healthy food or exercising for weight loss or weight control will change your life (or the lives of others) and/or if you regularly engage in fat talk or *grungie* talk, then eating disorder prevention and working with girls may not be for you. It is difficult to help girls accept their natural bodies if in our hearts we still believe that these bodies are wrong.

Trusting Yourself

Prevention is flexible. No two groups, presentations, classroom activities or discussions are exactly alike nor are any two practitioners. As women we learn from hands-on experience and from trial and error. If one activity or approach doesn't work, then we try another. When women are asked what they like best about working with girls most of them say it is the experience of learning about girls from the girls. Try looking at prevention with curiosity instead of approaching it with the fear of doing something wrong. Ask yourself what you learn from the girls and what you learn about yourself. This will help you trust yourself and give up your need to do everything perfectly the first time. As you become more comfortable working with girls you will gradually develop your own style and make the prevention strategies your own.

Practical Application:

- ➤ What three personal qualities do you bring to your work with girls?
- ➤ What two skills do you bring to your work with girls?
- ➤ What are you most curious about in working with girls?
- ➤ What would you find most difficult in working with girls?
- ➤ What would you need to feel more confident?

IMPLEMENTING PREVENTION IN OUR SCHOOLS

There are many ways in which prevention can be implemented in the schools. We can set aside time for prevention, we can implement specific prevention programs and we can integrate materials, skills and key elements into the existing curriculum. We can also take advantage of teachable moments. In the lower grades we can work with girls and boys together. Once students approach puberty we can work with the girls and boys separately. We can invite outside professionals or resource people into the school. Eating disorder prevention can involve students, staff, parents and administration and can make systemic changes in the school itself by creating a body-friendly environment that will nurture both girls and boys. Some schools may already be addressing the different components of prevention while some may be right at the beginning of the process. We need to respect where we are, identify what we need, and take small steps to implement change.

Practical Application:
You can use the exercises below by yourself or with others to assess
what is happening in your school and what needs to be done.

- ➤ *What's Happening in My School: A School Checklist* will help you assess what is happening in your school. Use *The Major Components of Prevention* and the *Basic Elements of Prevention* on pages 30-32 as a guide.

- ➤ *What's Happening in My School: An Individual Checklist* will help you assess your individual role and activities. It will help you articulate your needs and the barriers that stand in your way.

WHAT'S HAPPENING IN MY SCHOOL?

A SCHOOL CHECKLIST

In the list below check off each item that is addressed in your school, indicate in which grades this is addressed, into which part of the curriculum it is integrated and what program it is a part of:

	Is being addressed	Addressed in grades	Integrated into curriculum	Part of other program
Addressing the grungies	_____	_____	_____	_____
Puberty education	_____	_____	_____	_____
Metabolism /genetics	_____	_____	_____	_____
Eating for health /energy	_____	_____	_____	_____
Body awareness /appreciation	_____	_____	_____	_____
Media literacy	_____	_____	_____	_____
Media activism	_____	_____	_____	_____
Understanding gender	_____	_____	_____	_____
Encouraging self-expression	_____	_____	_____	_____
Building healthy relationships	_____	_____	_____	_____
Encouraging physical activity	_____	_____	_____	_____
Addressing bullying & teasing	_____	_____	_____	_____
Size Acceptance	_____	_____	_____	_____

Mark the appropriate answer below:

Yes_____No_____   Basic elements are integrated into everyone's practice.

Yes_____No_____   Basic elements are integrated into the curriculum.

What needs to be implemented in the school?_____

What are the barriers to this being done?_____

What small steps can be taken now?_____

WHAT'S HAPPENING IN MY SCHOOL?

AN INDIVIDUAL CHECKLIST

Check off the statements that apply to your experience with eating disorder prevention:

1. Yes____No____ Eating disorder prevention (*EDP*) is solely my responsibility.

2. Yes____No____ I work with someone else to implement *EDP* strategies.

3. Yes____No____ There is a team or committee in my school to address *EDP*.

4. Yes____No____ There are specific programs in place to address *EDP*.

5. Yes____No____ Our school is creating a body-friendly environment.

6. Yes____No____ I teach girls (and boys) about the grungies.

7. Yes____No____ I help girls fight the power of appearance.

8. Yes____No____ I encourage the acceptance of all shapes and sizes.

9. Yes____No____ I contribute to creating a body-friendly environment.

10. What I would like to do to address eating disorder prevention:

_____

_____

11. What I would like to see happening in my school:

_____

_____

12. The barriers or obstacles to this:

_____

_____

13. One small change that can be implemented now: _____

14. The skills I would need are:_____

_____

15. The support I would need: _____

_____

_____

Developing a Body-Friendly Environment*

One of the major goals of eating disorder prevention in the schools is the creation of a body friendly environment where:

➢ Girls and boys of all shapes and sizes feel good about their bodies.

➢ There is healthy communication and relationship building.

➢ There is no teasing.

➢ There are opportunities for physical activity and skill development.

➢ There are girl-only physical activities.

➢ There is a positive attitude towards food and a safe eating environment.

➢ Girls and boys are encouraged to speak out and their opinions are valued.

➢ Parents, teachers and students practice and reinforce the same skills.

Practical Application:

➢ *Imagine a Body-Friendly School* on page 43 will help you imagine what your school would be like if everybody was involved in making it a place where girls (and boys) felt good about their bodies and about themselves. Include the questions as part of your vision.

➢ *How Body-Friendly is Your Environment?* on page 44 will help you figure out if you have a body-friendly environment in your school. You can also use this quiz to assess organizations and your community. Score 2 for Often/Always, 1 for Sometimes and 0 for Never.

If you score between 23 and 28, you have a body-friendly environment. Keep up the good work!

If you score between 19 and 23, you have work to do. Go back to the assessment on page 41 and read the section on page 45 about *What Schools Can Do*. The strategies in the section on *Skills and Strategies* should help you.

If you score between 0 and 18, you have a problem. Your school is not a safe environment. You might want to consider professional training for staff and parents to help you set priorities and get started.

*The exercise on "How Body Friendly is Your Environment?" and the suggestions have been adapted from Rebecca Manley, M.S., Kirsten Reitter & Rachel Goren. Massachusetts Eating Disorder Association, Inc., 2002

IMAGINE A BODY-FRIENDLY SCHOOL...

...WHERE GIRLS FELT GOOD ABOUT THEIR BODIES AND THEMSELVES

Imagine you came into your school one morning and things had changed. The school was now a place where girls were able to express themselves. Their opinions were valued and encouraged. Their sizes and shapes were celebrated.

1. What changes would you notice on the playground?
2. What might you see on the walls, in the halls and in the classrooms?
3. How might participation in the classroom be different?
4. How might the curriculum change?
5. How would interaction in the staff room be different?
6. What would be available in the cafeteria?
7. How would lunch break encourage healthy eating?
8. How would P.E. classes be different?
9. What would the administration need to do to make the school safe for girls?
10. What would the staff need to do?
11. What would the parents need to do?
12. What would the students need to do?
13. What kind of help or support would they need?
14. Where can they get this help or support?

Girls learn best when they feel safe. This means their size and appearance are accepted and they are valued for who they are. In order to make this happen everyone involved with a school needs to be on board.

Adapted from *Focus On Bullying: A Prevention Program for Elementary School Communities*
British Columbia Ministry of Education and Ministry of the Attorney General

HOW BODY- FRIENDLY IS YOUR ENVIRONMENT?

1. People (teachers, staff and others who work with girls) don't criticize their own bodies.

Never   Sometimes   Often/Always

2. People are not constantly trying new fad diets or ways to lose weight.

Never   Sometimes   Often/Always

3. Teachers, coaches and others don't focus on Body Mass Index (BMI) or weigh students.

Never   Sometimes   Often/Always

4. There are many opportunities for physical activity.

Never   Sometimes   Often/Always

5. Weight loss and/or weight control is not a goal of physical activity.

Never   Sometimes   Often/Always

6. There are girl-only physical activities.

Never   Sometimes   Often/Always

7. The cafeteria serves has healthy foods besides fries and high fat food.

Never   Sometimes   Often/Always

8. There are no vending machines for candy and soda machines in the school.

Never   Sometimes   Often/Always

9. The students have more than 15-20 minutes to eat lunch.

Never   Sometimes   Often/Always

10. Students have the skills to deal with conflict, disagreements.

Never   Sometimes   Often/Always

11. There is a policy around teasing and bullying and the policy is enforced.

Never   Sometimes   Often/Always

12. There are pictures and posters of people of all shapes and sizes.

Never   Sometimes   Often/Always

13. There is training about prevention and about creating a body-friendly environment.

Never   Sometimes   Often/Always

14. There are resources and training for parents and the community about prevention
and creating a body friendly environment.

Never   Sometimes   Often/Always

Adapted from Rebecca Manley, M.S., Kirsten Reitter & Rachel Goren
Massachusetts Eating Disorder Association, Inc., 2002
[see page 42 for scoring]

WHAT SCHOOLS CAN DO

➤ Encourage parents, teachers and other school staff to explore their own beliefs about size and shape and to examine their own behaviors around food, weight and exercise. As adults we are role models for the girls we teach and work with. When we make comments about or criticize our own bodies or diet or talk about our diets, we teach these attitudes and behaviors to our students and also reinforce them.

➤ Get rid of the scales and the calipers and the Body Mass Index (BMI). There is absolutely no reason why you need to weigh your students or subject them to body fat analysis. If you think someone's weight is a health issue, refer that person to a physician who practices size acceptance.

➤ Provide a variety of physical activities. Make sure they are fun and all children have an opportunity to feel successful.

➤ Provide girl-only opportunities for physical activity and skill-building.

➤ Don't equate physical activity with weight loss or weight control. Place the emphasis on body awareness, strength and joy.

➤ Ensure that students have an adequate time to eat. Fifteen minutes for lunch is not enough time for them to digest their food.

➤ Try to provide a variety of choices in the cafeteria and make sure the calorie and fat content of the food are not displayed.

➤ Get rid of the vending and soda machines.

➤ Teach and model communication and conflict resolution skills, beginning in the earliest grades.

➤ Make sure all pictures and posters have people of all shapes and sizes including people who are fat.

➤ Enforce zero tolerance for teasing. Just as it is inappropriate to make racial, religious or homophobic comments, the same is true for body shape and size.

➤ Include students in planning a body-friendly environment and make sure that their voices are heard and their opinions are validated.

➤ Involve parents. They can reinforce the skills and key concepts that you teach and implement with the students.

➤ Provide ongoing professional training to parents and staff.

THE COLLABORATIVE MODEL OF PREVENTION[1]

Studies show the greater the change in body image attitudes in the wider school, family and social environment, the more likely that changes made by individuals will be supported and maintained. Dr. Niva Piran developed and implemented such a program in a ballet school in Toronto. She wanted to reduce the students' preoccupation with body weight and shape by creating an equitable and safe environment for adolescent girls.

Each year over a period of ten years Dr. Piran held meetings with the administration and staff of the ballet school She helped them identify factors within the school system that had a positive and negative impact on the students' body and self-image, examine their own attitudes towards body shape and weight and learn how to listen to students so they could hear and incorporate the feedback that they received.

Dr. Piran also facilitated small gender-defined focus groups for the students in each grade. Students explored and identified the dynamics in the school that contributed to feeling badly about their bodies and their selves. Discussions about body issues opened the door for students to talk about current experiences in their lives. Girls and young women spoke about how the school environment contributed to the feelings of constant pressure, unreasonable expectations and disregard for the individual. They talked about their difficulty in expressing their feelings and voicing their opinions in this atmosphere and about how powerless they felt when they were not heard. They spoke of harassment, violence and racism. As the girls talked about their problems in the safety of the group, solutions began to emerge.

The interventions that Dr. Piran suggested came out of the girls' knowledge and experiences and were enforced by the administration and staff. Guidelines were established around the way in which teachers and peers could and could not talk to each other and around comments that were made about their bodies. Because students felt supported they were able to confront staff members or each other when they experienced insults, criticisms or degradation.

By strengthening girls' relationships with each other, the school was able to facilitate healthy development and help girls maintain their voice at a time when they were most in danger of losing it. By strengthening girls' relationships with the administration and staff, girls felt supported and felt safe in talking about their feelings, experiences and opinions. The more empowered the girls felt, the less likely they were to redirect their feelings and experiences into the preoccupation with body shape and weight.

---

[1] Niva Piran. "The Reduction of Preoccupation with Body Weight and Shape in Schools: A Feminist Approach." in N. Piran, M.P. Levine, & C. Steiner-Adair, eds. *Preventing Eating Disorders: A Handbook of Interventions and Special Challenges.* Philadelphia: Taylor & Francis, 1999

In the ten years since the program was implemented only one student has been diagnosed with an eating disorder. Before the program began the average was one to two cases per year. Binge-eating decreased from 35% to 13%. Although 58% of seventh- and eighth-graders had reported dieting before the program, only 28% were dieting afterward. The standardized scores for tenth to twelfth-graders dropped from 58% to 16% in the eating disorder range.

Implementing the Collaborative Model of Prevention

All members of the school community—administrators, staff, parents, teachers and students—need to be involved so that everybody works toward a shared goal of creating a school culture that promotes positive body and self images among students. It helps to have a facilitator who can work with small groups and help small groups work with each other.

> ➢ Support needs to be provided for those students, parents and staff members who initiate change or who struggle with change.

> ➢ The facilitator has to be comfortable with the unstructured nature of the program. She needs to understand the developmental issues in girls' lives and must be comfortable sharing her values and experiences.

> ➢ Provision must be made to educate new members of the school community and to accommodate the leaving of current members so that the philosophy and vision remains the same.

> ➢ This same process can be used to address other issues such as bullying.

IMPLEMENTING PREVENTION IN THE COMMUNITY

Prevention is a community responsibility. It includes everybody involved with or who comes into contact with girls such as parents, relatives, teachers, older girls, guide leaders, coaches, neighbors, parks and recreation staff, camp counselors, and group and activity leaders. Even the corner grocery store is involved in prevention through the choices made in arranging and displaying magazines that promote thin and sexualized images of women and girls. Community-based prevention is about networking, team building, education, public awareness, service development and policy development. It is also about action. Everyone works together in order to fulfill a single goal—promoting and maintaining the healthy development of girls and thereby nurturing *girlpower*.

A community-based model of prevention will focus on creating a body-friendly environment. It will include prevention strategies that are integrated into the school curriculum and into activities that are conducted in the school either during or after school hours, into programs and resources offered by community centers, parks and recreation, Girl Guides, non-profits—any organizations that involve girls. Peer counseling is a good place for girls to teach other girls about the grungies and to encourage them to talk about what is underneath. Eating disorder prevention should also encompass parent education and in-service training for teachers, counselors, coaches, youth workers, church group leaders and other professional and lay people who are involved with girls.

Practical Application:

> *Building Integrated Community Teams* on page 49 will help you decide what kind of team you want and where you are in the process.

> *How Body-Friendly is Your Environment?* on page 44 can also help you assess your community.

> *Developing a Community-Based Model of Prevention* below will help you list the resources available in your community. Use Major Components Of Eating Disorder Prevention on pages 30-32 as a guide.

> *Developing a Community Map* on page 51 will help you clarify your goals and objectives.

Developing a Community-Based Model of Prevention

The more people and organizations involved in prevention, the greater the chance that it will be implemented in the community. Yet somebody (or rather some group of people) needs to take charge to ensure that prevention remains in the forefront of issues the community labels as important, to see that the energy doesn't dissipate and that everyone remains involved.

One of the best ways of ensuring eating disorder prevention takes place in your community is through teams. Teams enable people to open up the communication between the different members and organizations and to stop working in isolation. Remember that because addressing obesity is increasingly becoming a part of eating disorder prevention, it should also be addressed by your team.

Once you have decided on what kind of team you want, you need to decide who will be on it. Some teams are limited to teachers and to professionals in different agencies or organizations. Some include parents and/or youth or parents and youth. Including youth ensures girls and boys are given a voice and whatever resources or programs are developed are set in the context of their experiences.

BUILDING INTEGRATED COMMUNITY TEAMS

1. What kind of team would you want?

2. What kind of team already exists?

3. Who is included?

4. Who is missing?

5. What resources are available in your community to create or maintain this team?

6. What resources would you need?

7. What are the barriers to creating or maintaining this team?

8. Once you have created your team, how do you move ahead?

Beginning Stage – Developing Your Team

In the beginning stages of team development there may only be an informal network of contacts. You need to:

> Decide what kind of team you want and who is included, and what resources you would need.

> Recruit people who are also interested in building and working as a team.

> Identify a key person (or champion) who has a high level of interest and commitment and is willing to take on the responsibilities of leadership.

> Form a steering committee. Make sure the head of this committee is someone with good group facilitation and conflict resolution skills. (People come with different agendas and it is not uncommon for ideas to clash.)

> Develop a mechanism to handle conflict or anger.

> Find ways to stay connected.

Stage Two – Implementing the Mechanics

Once you have built your team it's time to set the mechanics in place:

> Consult with the community. What resources are available in the community? What changes or resources are needed to build your team?

> Discuss your philosophy. Make sure everyone on the team agrees with it.

> Define your goals and objectives. Make sure they are realistic. Developing a *community map* helps you envision what your community would be like if there were no more eating disorders and if you had a body-friendly environment. Do this exercise from time to time to ensure you are on track and to prevent your team from getting bogged down in negativity.

> Match your resources to your goals—ask yourselves whether you have the resources to achieve your goals.

> Decide on who you are going to target, e.g. service providers, parents, teachers, peer group leaders, churches, youth groups, hospital staff, etc.

> Make sure your messages are consistent and your language is clear. We often make the assumption everyone attributes the same meaning to a concept. However, healthy eating means something different to nutritionists than it does to women who have a history of dieting. Body image has a different meaning in the context of a weight loss group and in the context of public health.

> Build and nurture new partnerships.

> Learn from your own and others' experiences. Don't reinvent the wheel.

DEVELOPING A COMMUNITY-BASED PREVENTION MODEL

Many thanks to Barb Seed of Fraser Health Authority

Draw a pie-chart on a large piece of paper and divide it into slices labeled to correspond with categories of resources in your community. Begin with simple, broad categories. Brainstorm the categories as a group. For example: a 6-slice chart might contain these categories:

School (Curriculum)
Extra-curricular Activities
Parent Education
Professional Training & Inservice Education
Peer Counselling Resources
Community Services & Resources

Within each category list the resources currently available within your community. Use *Major Components of Eating Order Prevention* on page 31 and *How Body-friendly is Your Environment* on page 44 as guides. Don't forget to include any existing programs and organizations that include girls, and the school curriculum itself. Invite representatives from these sectors to participate in your enterprise.

Add resources which may not currently exist but need to be developed and underline them. Older members of your group may recall programs and opportunities that once worked effectively in the past but no longer exist. Use your imagination. Now you have a starting point for discussion of what your community still needs and how you can work to make this happen.

Create a Venn diagram chart of overlapping circles of influence to help pinpoint which professionals/organizations are most influential in which areas. This will help you assess which organizations within the community have the best resources for developing particular programs and supporting them over time.

You might consider applying this same technique to prevention programs within the community to address a broad range of health and social risks. It helps in designing schemes for effective long-term program delivery and in dividing out the responsibilities to different sectors of the community for staffing and managing them.

Beware of becoming overly sophisticated—an effective, long-term prevention strategy can be as simple as an ongoing series of 15-minute presentations reminding girls how to interpret and diffuse the *grungies*.

DEVELOPING A COMMUNITY MAP

A *community map* helps teams who are just beginning (and teams who are getting bogged down) to develop a more coherent vision.

Materials: flip chart / felt pens / Post-it notes

Describe the answers to the following on the flip chart:

Part I:

Imagine your community successfully <u>stopping</u> eating disorders and creating a body-friendly environment.

➢ What services would need to be in place to achieve this?

➢ What activities would need to be offered?

➢ What skills would need to be taught to volunteers and professionals?

Part II:

➢ Put a **check mark** by all the activities and services currently in place.

➢ Put an **x** by the activities and skills that individuals can address in their own practice.

➢ **Circle** the activities that require group effort.

Part III:

➢ Give each person 3 Post-It notes. Ask them to prioritize the top three services/activities/skills from the community map that they believe the group could address. Tally all of the votes. The activity receiving the most votes would be the first priority that the group might address.

➢ Set up a meeting to develop action. List who should be involved, the time frame, and whatever else might be necessary.

➢ Determine who will be in charge.

➢ Determine how you will stay connected afterwards to address the next problem, etc.

Stage Three – Assessing Your Effectiveness

From time to time you need to stop and assess your effectiveness. Use the following questions as a guide:

➢ What was achieved?

➢ Did your team meet its objectives?

➢ Were there any unexpected objectives?

➢ How could your meetings, implementation be improved or built on?

➢ What's needed next?

➢ What other people should be involved?

Stage Four – Renewing and Revitalizing Existing Teams

Teams often tend to bog down after they have been together for a while. Some difficulties include: lack of energy and time, lack of community awareness, practitioners working in isolation, lack of nonprofessionals on the team, lack of knowledge about the process involved in working with different community groups, lack of focus because of conflicting goals or the overwhelming number of needs in the community, lack of resources and turnover of members. To renew and revitalize your existing team:

➢ Acknowledge what the group has accomplished. A timeline chart helps remind people what the group has done and where it is going.

➢ Review the purpose and vision of the group and the needs of the community.

➢ Take on one project at a time.

➢ Keep the projects or group tasks simple.

➢ Keep the responsibility evenly spread out so that one person doesn't take it all on.

➢ Evaluate your projects.

➢ Acknowledge and celebrate your achievements.

➢ Begin and end meetings on time.

➢ Make sure everyone has a chance to speak and everyone feels heard.

➢ Deal with any conflict that may arise either in the group or outside of the group before the next meeting.

➢ Find a way to stay connected.

Encountering Barriers

Whether you are just beginning to develop your team or you have one that is well-established, you are going to run into barriers. Regardless of the importance of prevention, it is the 'poor cousin' on the continuum of disordered eating/eating disorders. It has less money and less of a voice in deciding how resources designated for eating disorders are allocated. If you are in a rural or remote community you may find you lack access to and availability of services that are available in urban areas.

Regardless of the initial enthusiasm, time constraints often become an issue with team members. It takes a lot of time to network. As teams develop, they often have no mechanisms in place to deal with conflicts or with the clash of opinions that arise. When this happens, meetings begin to feel unsafe and people stay away. Many teams, especially in rural and remote communities have to deal with attrition and with transience—with people leaving and new people coming in. None of these barriers are insurmountable, but they do need to be addressed as they arise.

Keeping Your Team Together

Now that your team is up and running, you need to find ways to ensure the commitment of team members to keep the team together.

> ➢ Revisit your goals and objectives to ensure that they are clear and concrete. Nothing causes people to lose interest faster than muddy goals and objectives.

> ➢ Assign tasks so that everyone remains interested. Make sure these tasks are simple and achievable. People drop out when they feel overwhelmed or underutilized.

> ➢ Discuss the challenges and issues that you are facing on a regular basis.

> ➢ Designate a chair to maintain cohesiveness and coordination between groups. Rotate the chair to ensure that the work load is spread around.

> ➢ Network, network, network!

Moving Ahead

Once you have established your team and have addressed the barriers, you need to talk about how you are going to move ahead in order to get your message across and generate action. Often when I do professional training the sponsors also organize an evening seminar in the community for parents, people who work with girls and girls themselves. After my presentation there is an opportunity for people to network, and for teams to showcase their resources, publicize what they are doing, recruit volunteers and mobilize the community.

ACQUIRING PREVENTION SKILLS

This section addresses the body issues and life/self issues that make up the major components of eating disorder prevention and describes the basic elements you can integrate into your practice. All of the skills and strategies in this section can be adapted for use in early intervention, in addressing obesity, and for use with boys. I have indicated which risk factors each section or topic addresses.

grungies — When Girls Feel Fat

Risk Factors Addressed:
Loss of Voice
Changes in Relationships
Body Dissatisfaction

It's hard to grow up female today without ever feeling fat. Fat talk (*grungie* talk) has become a kind of shorthand for communication between women and girls in our society. Instead of talking about real issues and concerns, girls say "I feel fat," or "look at my thighs" or "if only I was thinner…" We reply "no you're not." They say "yes I am" and we proceed into a frustrating circular argument. We feel they are not listening to us and they feel unheard. Instead of responding to what is probably an indication of distress and then engaging in a meaningful conversation, the connection between us is broken.

When girls talk about 'feeling fat' they are usually not referring to their size. Thin girls feel fat and fat girls feel fat. Nobody feels fat all the time. If at two o'clock, for example, someone felt fine and at two-thirty she felt fat, it was not because she swallowed a watermelon. The change that took place was not physical. It was emotional and was in response to a specific stressor or trigger.

Girls feel fat and learn to speak in fat talk as a by-product of their socialization. This is because as girls grow up they are socialized to repress their feelings and internalize their distress, to draw their pain into themselves. Instead of being able to address situations directly, they learn to blame themselves. They ask "What's wrong with me? What did I do?" They talk about being angry with themselves. They worry about what people think about them, and try to accommodate others at the expense of themselves. They give themselves *grungies*.

Grungies are our negative voice. They are the things
we say that make us feel badly about ourselves.

Underneath every *grungie* is the story of a real
feeling or experience waiting to find expression.

The most common *grungies* are 'fat', 'ugly' and 'stupid'.

When girls can't express their feelings or talk about what's bothering them directly, they learn to do so indirectly by learning to speak in code. One way of doing this is through the *grungies*—a term coined to describe the negative voice girls develop. Girls tell themselves that they 'feel fat or stupid or ugly' when they feel angry or insecure or lonely, or experience any other feelings they don't recognize or are discouraged from expressing, or when they don't have the language skills to talk about their experiences, or are otherwise prohibited from doing so. Because girls are socialized to value themselves according to how they look, and because fat is considered bad by our society, many girls 'feel fat.' Focusing on body size becomes a way of turning concerns about something real on the inside into something artificial on the outside that seems easier to manage.

It's up to us to help girls become aware of their grungies and teach them to decode the language of fat by telling the stories that lie underneath their grungies. If we fail to do this then girls will continue to associate the discomfort of their feelings with 'fat' and not with the underlying stressor. They act on this discomfort by trying to get rid of the fat through dieting—rather than by addressing and dealing with the original trigger.

Practical Application:

You can use the *GRUNGIE THOUGHTS TEST* on page 57 with girls as a way of leading into a discussion about the grungies or as part of intervention with girls who are already experimenting with eating disorder behaviors.

- ➢ Score 1-26 and grungies are probably not an issue.
- ➢ Score between 27-60 and it sounds like the beginning of a problem.
- ➢ A score between 61-80 suggests you might need help with your problems.

Use the test a second time as a follow-up after you have worked with girls to see what changes have taken place.

THE *GRUNGIE* THOUGHTS TEST

In the last week, how often have you had each of these thoughts?

0	1	2	3	4
Never	Sometimes	Moderately often	Often	Always (or almost always)

1._____My life is lousy because of how I look.

2._____If I was thinner I would feel more confident in my work.

3._____I feel fat.

4._____Why can't I ever look good?

5._____Other people look like they are 'together.'

6._____I can never do anything right.

7._____I must lose weight.

8._____People won't like me because I'm fat.

9._____Other people are more articulate, talented, compassionate, etc.

10._____When things don't work out for me I feel stupid.

11._____If I was more interesting I would have more friends.

12._____If I was thinner I would do the things I've always wanted to do.

13._____I'll never be attractive.

14._____I hate my body.

15._____Everyone here knows more than I do.

16._____Everybody else is thinner than me.

17._____I always feel fat when I am with people who are thinner than me.

18._____I'm so boring. I never have anything interesting to say.

19._____When I make a mistake I feel stupid.

20._____Whenever I'm in a new situation I feel fat or stupid.

Teaching Girls About the Grungies

Years ago, after I first began to work with girls and women with weight preoccupation I went back to Montreal to visit my family. I was also asked to be on my very first radio call-in talk show while I was there. My mother was going to be listening along with my relatives and friends. When I woke up the morning of the talk show my excitement was rapidly replaced by a grungie. Not only did I feel fat but I kept on telling myself if I was thinner, the radio talk show would be a success. When I got beneath my grungie I discovered how scared I was. What if I didn't know the right answer when someone called in? What if I had nothing to say? Once I started to talk about the fear, I was able to move past it.

In some of the professional training sessions I facilitate I often simulate a 'grungie group' as an experiential way to teach skills. Four or five brave women volunteer to form a semi-circle in front of the larger group. I use the process described below to help them become aware of their own grungies and to encourage them to tell the stories that are underneath.

The women speak about their feelings of inadequacy mothering teenage girls. They speak about their difficulties in setting boundaries at home and at work, about their need to please other people, about problems they are having in their relationships, about their inability to express their anger, their guilt in wanting time alone for themselves, their grief over the breakdown of relationships and the loss of parents. In the telling of their stories, these women validate their life experiences both for themselves and others.

Workshop participants find the grungie group very valuable because it gives them an opportunity to identify and experience their own grungies and to understand the relationship between having a grungie and the fact there is actually a real feeling and situation underneath. Exploring real issues helps people acquire a sense of control. Talking about them to others validates them—which is far more rewarding than the dead end of 'feeling fat'. You might find it helpful to work on your own grungies before or at the same time you are trying it out with girls.

When a Girl has been *'Hit by a Grungie'*

Help her pay attention to what information she is telling about herself. Girls use grungies in different ways. Some say, "I feel fat." Others say things like "If I were smarter or thinner..." or "I'm so unattractive...." or "I'm such a loser." There are also other things that girls tell themselves when they dump on themselves. Some girls give themselves a grungie when they constantly feel guilty, and blame themselves for things that are beyond their control. The first step is helping girls recognize which ones are truly theirs and when they are using them.

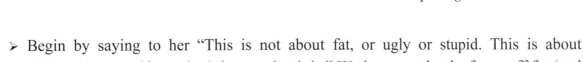

➢ Begin by saying to her "This is not about fat, or ugly or stupid. This is about something else, even if you don't know what it is." We have to take the focus off fat (and ugly and stupid, etc.) before girls can discover what they are really feeling. Every time a girl says she feels fat, what she is really saying is "I don't like myself"—and that is learned behavior. It is also a way of speaking in code.

➢ Even when girls don't know what lies underneath their grungies, the very fact they are aware of them takes away the grungie's power—because girls no longer respond to the situation by addressing the fat instead of the feeling. Ask her what happened to make her feel fat when she didn't feel 'fat' twenty minutes ago.

➢ Help her look at the context. Girls tend to talk in global terms such as 'always' and 'never' so make it very specific. Ask her what she was doing when she was hit by the grungie. What day was it? What time of the day was it? What was she thinking about? Was there anything she didn't want to do? Was she feeling angry, disappointed, insecure or lonely? Was she having conflict with any of her friends? These are feelings and situations most girls have difficulty dealing with.

➢ Ask her to describe the circumstances or context when she felt fat, ugly or stupid—but this time leave out the grungie. Ask her to replace it with a real feeling, something other people can relate to. For example, the first time she might say "I woke up in the morning and felt fat." Now ask her what she would feel if she didn't feel fat. (Stupid, awful, confused, depressed are not allowed!) She may respond by saying "I woke up in the morning and felt like I didn't want to go to school." If she can't get to what's underneath her grungie encourage her not to give up. Remind her it takes time to make the connection between feeling fat or ugly or stupid, and something else that is lurking underneath.

➢ Sometimes girls say they feel fat but there isn't anything underneath it. They say it's because their clothes don't fit or they ate too much. Remember feeling fat always has a negative connotation and is always used as a way of putting ourselves down. Talking about how you feel about being fat is not the same as 'feeling fat'. When you talk about how you feel about a specific thing there is engagement. The other person can relate to what you are saying and can add her own experiences. 'Feeling fat' is a dead end.

➢ If girls tell you they feel fat all of the time (as in the case with girls who have eating disorders), just focus on one or two specific incidents. Don't give up. Remember the reason girls speak in code is because some things are just too difficult or scary to say out loud.

➤ When she does finally have a sense of what's underneath her grungie it's important for her to know she doesn't have to do anything directly about it. Lots of times it is just too scary and perhaps even inappropriate. She doesn't have to confront her teacher or yell at her best friend. Because our society is so focused on instant solutions, girls sometimes think they have to act immediately every time they have a feeling. We cannot expect girls to take action when they are not ready, or don't have the proper skills or support, or are really scared. But we must guard against their silencing what they know and feel.

➤ Don't repress, express! Many girls think the only way they can express their feelings is directly to the source. We need to teach them other creative ways of telling their stories and of getting their feelings out and provide them with opportunities to practice. When girls don't express their feelings, the feelings go looping around and around inside their heads and they end up turning into grungies. There are many ways for girls to express their feelings indirectly:

- They can find a private place and just talk out loud about what is bothering them.
- They can say things like "I'm so angry with Sally because she forgot my birthday. I just want to…"
- They can speak to the person symbolically without that person being there, by saying "I'm so angry with you Sally because…"
- They can write it out or draw a picture.
- They can hold a *DEAD FLOWER* CEREMONY *(*see page 61*)*

➤ When girls express their feelings, we need to validate them. They need to know they have a right to the way they feel and they are probably not alone in how they feel. This is a good time for schmoozing.

Once girls have expressed their feelings, we can begin to look at steps they may take to resolve the situation. If we do this too early, girls feel we are telling them what to do. Girls have to be reminded to take baby steps and only when they are ready. Sometimes they have to spend a lot of time over and over again on the feelings before they can move on to the resolution.

Girls need a lot of support in helping to identify and then deal with their grungies. Be patient. It takes time and experience to elicit the kind of information that is usually underneath—like peeling back the layers of an onion. If they can't figure it out right away, it's not because you've done something wrong, but because they don't have enough practice. Remember the process is just as valuable as the goal. Just thinking about grungies and what may be underneath breaks the obsessive cycle that happens when girls feel fat.

HOLDING A *DEAD FLOWER CEREMONY*

Materials: dead flowers *(or tissues)* / pens / garbage can

We often give people live flowers to show our love and appreciation of them. Why not send them dead flowers (symbolically) when we feel angry, hurt or disappointed! You can use real flowers or make the flowers out of tissues (or out of paper).

Let the girls know that sometimes when we get angry with people or feel hurt and disappointed it's too scary for us to tell them directly how we are feeling. If we keep the feelings inside, they turn into *grungies*—so we need to express them. A safe way to do that is to talk to the person symbolically when they are not actually there and can't respond. (Talking *about* someone doesn't have the same impact as talking *to* them.)

Have each girl think of someone she is angry with. If anger is hard for some girls, then use words such as annoyed, just a little bit upset, etc. Ask them to think about what they would say to the person if they were not afraid of hurting them or being hurt themselves. If you are using tissues/paper, have them write what they would like to say on the 'flowers'. Remind them that nobody is going to look at their flower.

The *Dead Flower Ceremony*:

➢ Place a garbage can in the center of the room.

➢ Have each girl stand in front of the garbage can, say out loud what she would like to say to the person and then throw the flower and her feelings into the can.

➢ Once she has said what she needs to, she can let the feelings go.

➢ If you are doing this exercise with a large group have the girls simultaneously and silently say what they would like to say and then throw the flowers and feelings away.

One grade 9 group I facilitated was held in June so the girls were able to bring real dead flowers. The ceremony went over so well the next week each girl came to the group carrying a full bag of dead flowers! The garbage can over-flowed that day with feelings that would otherwise have remained inside.

BUILDING COMMUNICATION SKILLS

Risk Factors Addressed:
Loss of Voice
Changes in Relationships
Self-Esteem
Teasing

Girls grow up in *relationship* to other people. The strength and integrity of these connections help them define their sense of self and provide them with a sense of well-being. Before puberty, girls trust in their abilities to express and resolve differences between themselves. They are able to speak their minds directly because they do not fear that what they say might contribute to the end of relationships as they know and experience them.

As girls move into adolescence they are socialized to hold back what they think and feel in order to avoid hurting another person's feelings. When girls can't be frank with one another their relationships begin to change, and they experience the dark side of friendship.

In elementary school, girls tease and exclude one another and secrets emerge. When girls have no way of resolving conflict, they feel anxious about the stability of their friendships and internalize their distress. Communication and conflict resolution skills are a major part of eating disorder prevention because they help girls develop and maintain healthy relationships and validate their right to speak and be heard. They also help girls deal with teasing and bullying.

Communication

Communication is any behavior that carries a message that is perceived by someone else. It can be verbal or non-verbal and intended or unintended. When my cat Theodora sits beside her dish, the non-verbal message she is sending is quite clear. The recipient can receive the message and perceive it accurately or inaccurately. The sender needs to be able to deal with the response in a way that continues to engage the other person. Good communication involves:

> Sending and receiving messages in such a way that both participants can understand them.

> Leaving us feeling connected even though we might disagree on the subject.

> Leaving the door open for negotiation and resolution.

> Taking responsibility for ourselves by using 'I' messages.

> Actively listening to the response instead of planning a defense, or attacking or withdrawing.

Passive Behavior and Communication

Because girls are socialized to be *kind* and *nice* and to please others, they learn a passive style of communication that is indirect and is characterized by avoidance of anything that might resemble conflict. Some people go to great lengths in their passive communication. A woman I know worked odd hours and liked to spend her time at home alone. Because she was afraid to tell her neighbors not to come over, she kept her coat near the door. When the bell rang, she put her coat on, opened the door and said, "Oh, I was just going out." Not everyone is so creative. Often girls who learn to communicate passively suffer in silence, cannot openly express their feelings or opinions and therefore don't ever get their needs met.

Aggressive Behavior and Communication

An aggressive style of communication is characterized by a loud voice and intimidating and demanding behavior. Saying: "Stop bugging me. You always interrupt when I am reading" is an example of aggressive communication. Aggressive communication tends to be associated with boys who are encouraged to express their anger and who learn to externalize their distress by blaming others. When girls are aggressive they are often labeled as 'bitches' or girls who are not nice.

Passive-Aggressive Behavior and Communication

Passive/aggressive style combines the worst traits of passiveness and aggressiveness. Girls and boys who have difficulty expressing anger and want to avoid conflict seem to agree with others or acquiesce on the surface, but later express hostility in indirect, mean and sneaky ways. An example of passive-aggressive behavior is having someone say: "I can see it bothered you that I wore your sweater, I won't do it again"—and later put your sweater in the dryer where it shrinks. Because you never quite know how they feel nor what they will do, passive-aggressive characters often inspire mistrust in others.

Assertive Behavior and Communication

Assertive behavior is a combination of what we say and how we say it. Being assertive means being clear and direct about what we want and what we think while at the same time respecting the rights of others. Saying: "I would like to finish this chapter in my book because I am at the exciting part. Then I will talk to you" is an example of assertive behavior. We use assertive behavior to stick up for our rights, to let people know what we want and to let them know what we will or will not do.

Practicing Assertive Behavior

- ➢ Stand tall.
- ➢ Look at the person.
- ➢ Use a strong, clear voice.
- ➢ Say the person's name.
- ➢ Describe the behavior or the problem.
- ➢ Set a limit or tell the person to stop.
- ➢ Use 'I' messages.

DEALING WITH CONFLICT

It's impossible to go through life without ever experiencing conflict. No matter how good the friendship or relationship or how well we think we understand the other person, there will be times when we have differences. We may want different things, or have different perspectives on situations, or we may have made assumptions about the other person that are wrong, or we've said something (perhaps unintentionally) that has caused the other person to feel hurt or angry.

Conflict can be a healthy part of a friendship when we have good communication skills. When we resolve conflict successfully and when each person feels heard and validated, we feel closer to the other person—not further away as we may fear. However, when we don't know how to deal with conflict we tend to keep silent because of our fear of rejection. We move away from the other person. She senses our withdrawal, but wanting to keep the peace, responds by moving away from us. In the end our worse fear materializes—our friendship is at risk because of the rift that develops between us.

When we can't deal with conflict directly, we often do so indirectly. We resort to passive or passive-aggressive behavior because we are afraid if we say what we feel we will be rejected. Sometimes anger about the issue that created the conflict builds up and bubbles over so that we react in an aggressive manner. This causes defensiveness or withdrawal in the other person. The exercises on page 68 will help you teach girls skills and allow them to practice these skills so that they can become assertive and can deal with conflict in a direct, healthy and respectful way.

Rules for Good Communication and for Dealing with Conflict

> Identify the problem.

> Define the problem as a mutual one.

> Attack the problem—not the person.

> Don't make assumptions about the other person.

> Check out your perceptions.

> Practice 'I' messages.

> Listen with an open mind.

> Stay with the specific issue.

> Avoid generalizations such as 'you always !' or 'you never!'

> Avoid name-calling, blaming, putting the other person down.

> Treat the other person with respect.

Giving Feedback

When we deal with conflict we need to know how to give feedback in such a way that we let the other person know how her behavior affects us. We have to phrase what we say so she will not feel blamed or criticized and will listen. We need to have the other person respond in such a way that we know she understands how we feel. This makes us feel heard and lets us move past the conflict. The acronym **WIN** helps us remember how to give feedback.

WIN stands for: **W**hen you…….

I feel

I **N**eed

Example: Your friend watches what you eat and keeps pressuring you to diet. Every time you ask her to stop she backs off for a while and then begins again. You want to be friends with her but you also want to be in charge of what you eat.

"**WHEN YOU** watch what I eat and keep telling me to diet **I FEEL** you are taking away my choices about what is right for me and that I am not in control of my own food. **I NEED** you to stop commenting on what I eat."

If you feel more comfortable reversing the order, begin with I FEEL, WHEN YOU, then I NEED. That's also a good way of giving feedback. Practice until you find a style that is comfortable for you.

Giving Feedback

- ➤ Let the other person know you are not trying to criticize or blame her for anything but want to tell her about a situation where you felt uncomfortable.

- ➤ Describe the behavior so the other person has an idea of what she did that made you react.

- ➤ Be specific. Talk about just the one incident.

- ➤ Describe the feelings that you had.

- ➤ Use "I" statements.

- ➤ Describe the outcome or effect this behavior had on you.

- ➤ Let the person know what you want from them.

Receiving Feedback

Good communication means giving the other person a chance to respond. She may not see things in the same way you do. She may feel hurt or angry. Her first reaction may be a feeling of being blamed or criticized. We need to remember hurt is a part of the repertoire of feelings that everyone comes equipped with, and that hurt is a normal reaction when people see or experience things differently. We need to give the other person time to take in what we say, think about it, and then respond. Good communication doesn't mean taking feelings away from the other person or taking back our own feelings in order to make her feel better. It means letting her know we understand how she can feel that way even if the way we experience or see things is different from they way she does and then asking her if she can see how we felt.

Example: You have told your friend how you feel when she tells you what to eat and not eat. At first she feels criticized and feels you don't trust her. She tells you she has your best interests at heart and wants you to be thin. Instead of feeling guilty, you say:

"I'm not trying to hurt you or criticize you by what I'm saying, I just want you to know how I feel. I can see how you are thinking about my welfare. Can you see how I felt about your telling me to diet?"

Dealing with the Response to Feedback

➢ Listen with curiosity. Do not try to plan your response in advance.

➢ Ask yourself if there are any parts to her story or to her response where you can see how she might have felt the way that she did.

➢ Acknowledge her feelings. If she feels hurt or angry, don't try to take her feelings away from her. Your guilt doesn't do her any good.

➢ Let her know you can see how she feels the way that she does. You might not have felt the same way, but you can respect how she feels.

➢ Use "I" statements.

➢ If necessary, tell your side of the story again and ask her if she can see how you felt the way that you did.

Roses and Onions

Sometimes we feel uncomfortable launching right into telling someone how that person's behavior makes us feel. It's hard not to see giving feedback as telling someone 'bad things.' Some people find it helpful to begin by saying something 'good' or giving positive feedback—giving *roses*. Then they tell the other person about what is bothering them—giving them *onions*. Girls often find that talking about 'roses' and 'onions' is easier to conceptualize and much less scary than thinking or talking about giving feedback. As well, sometimes people are more receptive to feedback if we establish something positive about them first.

'Yes, but...' Making Ourselves Heard

Sometimes when we give feedback, the person responds with "Yes, but you..." We then defend ourselves and we lose sight of the message that we are trying to put across.

Example: You have told your friend how you feel when she tries to get you to diet. She feels criticized and feels you don't trust her.

Friend: "It's not my fault. I am doing it for your own good. If you didn't eat so much you would be thinner and would be more popular."

You: "I don't believe in dieting. If you ate normally you wouldn't be so obsessed with food."

Friend: "You think you're so perfect. Everybody knows that you..."

You: "Well you..."

When people are defensive and answer, "Yes, but…" it helps to respond by repeating our message word for word. We may have to do this several times until the other person begins to hear us. We can acknowledge she also may have an issue, but we can only deal with it after we have resolved ours. (This is a good skill to teach girls when they are being teased.) Use the instructions for the other communications exercises to practice dealing with 'Yes, but….'"

Example: You have told your friend how you feel when she tries to get you to diet. She feels criticized and feels you don't trust her.

Friend: "It's not my fault. I am doing it for your own good. If you didn't eat so much you would be thinner and would be more popular."

You: I can see where you are worried about my eating and want to do things for my own good. We can talk about what that means but only after we have resolved my feelings about your telling me what to do. **WHEN YOU** watch what I eat and keep telling me to diet **I FEEL** that you are taking away my choices about what is right for me and that I am not in control of my own food. **I NEED** you to stop commenting on what I eat."

Friend: "You think you're so perfect. Everybody knows that you…"

You: "**WHEN YOU** watch what I eat and keep telling me to diet **I FEEL** that you are taking away my choices about what is right for me and that I am not in control of my own food. **I NEED** you to stop commenting on what I eat."

Friend: "I'm sorry I'll try hard to not do it again."

Practicing Communication Skills:

➤ Divide the girls into groups of three or four. Ask each small group to share with each other past situations where they would have wanted to be assertive or give feedback or deal with defensiveness. Describe the situations on flip chart paper.

➤ Have the group choose one situation. Have one girl be the assertive party, one girl be the responder and the rest of the girls be the audience. Remember that girls can opt out if they are not comfortable role-playing.

➤ Have the group do this again with someone else's situation. Do the same exercise to practice giving feedback and dealing with 'yes, but…'

➤ You can adapt this to one-to-one situations. If you are working with someone Individually, have her identify a situation and take turns role playing both parts with her.

OUR BODIES

Risk Factors Addressed:
Body Dissatisfaction
Being Fat
Self Esteem

When I am motivated to move my body by negativity, I carry that negative energy with me and I will choose to move because there is something wrong with me, because I need to change, because I am not good enough.

When I am motivated with positive energy, I will choose to move my body for MYSELF because I AM worthy, because I AM capable and because I deserve to participate in this life affirming action.

When I listen to MY body, it is a gift to MY self.

Denise Hodgins, Vancouver Island Eating Disorders Association

We only get one body. At times it is our area of greatest joy. Look at babies as they kick and stretch. Watch little girls as they run and jump. See the pleasure they get from using their bodies and moving around. Imagine the feeling of satin and velvet on your skin. Feel the warmth of the sun. Remember how you've felt after you've received a massage. *Body image* is a term used to describe all of the factors that influence how we perceive our bodies and how we feel about them.

Body image involves:

➤ How you see or picture yourself.

➤ How you feel others perceive you.

➤ What you believe about your physical appearance.

➤ How you feel about your body.

➤ How you feel in your body.

➤ How you move in your body.

Other factors also affect how you perceive and feel about your body:

➤ Physical changes—such as puberty, menopause and pregnancy.

➤ Injuries or disabilities.

➤ Sexual and physical abuse.

➤ Sexual harassment, racism and homophobia.

The Ideal Body—an Historical Perspective

The greatest impact on how we perceive our bodies and feel about them comes from the pressure we experience to conform to prevailing social values. The obsession with body shape and size is not a new phenomenon. Throughout history, society has worshipped an ideal image of the female body. While women themselves might have been relegated to second-class or inferior status because of who they were, those who came closest to the physical ideal were revered and given elevated status just because of how they looked.

In the 1890s, the famous English actress Lillian Russell was considered a great beauty—and weighed 90 kilograms (200 pounds). Her flawless skin and plump figure made her more desirable than the also popular but skinny French actress Sarah Bernhardt. Artist Charles Dana Gibson's paintings made at this time of tall, athletic, self-confident 'Gibson Girls' represented voluptuousness in their corseted hourglass figures. During the 1920s, a time of greater opportunity and freedom for women, the 'Flapper' achieved a flat-chested, slim-hipped, and androgynous look by binding her breasts to minimize her curves and by dieting—the beginning of a practice that women continue to use to change their body shape and size to meet an ideal. Then came the Depression and World War II. As men entered the armed forces, society's image changed. The ideal woman was now full-bodied. Her big shoulders made her strong enough to take her place in the work-force. She also had the actress Betty Grable's shapely legs.

In the 1950s, Marilyn Monroe became the ideal woman because she was voluptuous and curvaceous. Her full breasts were a symbol of both sexuality and motherhood in a society that was encouraging women to get out of the workforce and back into the home. When Barbie made her debut in 1959, she introduced us to an ideal body that was physically impossible for a real woman to achieve—but which we are still striving for. In the 60s and 70s, the women's movement came into being. So did Twiggy—a thin waif-like model who introduced the anorexic look. Actress Jane Fonda intensified our obsession with fitness in 1982 by bringing out the first in what would become a never-ending string of celebrity exercise videos.

Madonna introduced underwear as outerwear in 1985 and in 1990 the sickly, bone-thin supermodel took her place in our definition of beauty. Today the ideal woman is big breasted, thin and has muscle tone. Girls can no longer strive for the perfect body by dieting. They have to go under the knife in order to have *perfected* bodies that can only be created by cosmetic surgery. No matter how girls look, they feel that something about them is intrinsically wrong or broken and has to be fixed.

Fluctuations in the body ideal tell us about women's place in society and about the economics of different times. When life was more precarious and resources scarce, fat was highly desirable because it represented health and wealth. A woman who was fat was able to bear children. A man with a fat wife was seen to be rich and therefore respected. In times of prosperity, thinness was associated with idleness. The less a woman did that was productive, the more it reflected on a man's ability to provide for her. Just think about Scarlett O'Hara lacing up her corsets in *Gone With the Wind*.

In times of social change and opportunity for women, body ideals become more restrictive. The more women obsess about their bodies, the less likely they are to get on with their lives and the easier it is to keep them silent. The more energy required to achieve an ideal body, the less time women have to contribute to and take their place in the world. The more opportunity that exists for women, the smaller or thinner woman are pressured to be (and therefore become insubstantial and invisible). As opportunities become restricted for men to define themselves by what they do, the greater the emphasis on building bigger and more muscular bodies.

The Pressure to be Thin

Until girls are about 8 years old, they tend to feel good about their bodies (unless they have been physically or sexually abused, or are differently-abled or fat). At eight, they are as tall as boys and are often stronger because they weigh more. Because they are relatively free from the influences of societal pressures at this time in their lives, they have a positive body image. That is, their experience of their bodies is congruent with their perceptions of their bodies.

As girls approach puberty they receive clear messages from their families and from our society that in order to be valued they need to be attractive and that to be attractive they need to be thin. Girls are socialized to deny acceptance of their changing bodies. At a time when they most need food, many girls begin to restrict what they eat because they are afraid of getting fat. As their hips get bigger and they accumulate the fat necessary for them to develop as sexual women, and as the discrepancy between the societal norms of beauty and their biological and genetic heritage widens, many girls feel that their bodies are abnormal. As they navigate through adolescence they are taught there is something wrong with them if they are not constantly trying to improve by changing their bodies. They are also taught if they try hard enough they, too, can be thin.

Practical Application:

Take the *BODY IMAGE TEST* on the next page. If you score between 0-12, body image is not an issue with you, 12-18 sounds like the beginning of a problem, 19-24 means that body image concerns and grungies are taking up a big part of your life, 25-36 looks like you might need some outside help.

THE BODY IMAGE TEST

Adapted from (oxygen)thriveonline   http://www.thriveonline.com/shape/wgames/gen/shape.bodyimage.html

How healthy is your image of your body? Find out how your body image measures up:

Never   Sometimes   Often   Always

_____   _____   _____   _____   1. When I look in the mirror, the image reflected back to me is not who I want to be.

_____   _____   _____   _____   2. I'd rather shop for pet food than for clothing.

_____   _____   _____   _____   3. I go through at least three outfit changes when I get dressed and I'm still not happy.

_____   _____   _____   _____   4. I never exercise or participate in sports unless I can wear baggy sweats.

_____   _____   _____   _____   5. I think my body is ugly and I'm sure that others think so too.

_____   _____   _____   _____   6. When I'm out with friends I feel everyone else is more attractive than I am.

_____   _____   _____   _____   7. When I go out with my family, I can't help wondering if people think I missed out on the 'good-looking' genes.

_____   _____   _____   _____   8. I compare myself with others to see if they are heavier than I am. It's all I can think about when I'm with another person.

_____   _____   _____   _____   9. I am so self-conscious about how I look that it's hard to enjoy activities like going out to dinner or to the movies with friends.

_____   _____   _____   _____   10. Being unhappy with my appearance preoccupies my mind.

_____   _____   _____   _____   11. I know that my thoughts about my body and appearance are negative, but I can't stop them.

_____   _____   _____   _____   12. I believe dieting will change my life forever.

BODY AWARENESS AND APPRECIATION

During adolescence girls step outside themselves to judge their bodies, focusing on the specific parts that they don't like. They hate their stomachs, their thighs are too big, their arms are flabby, etc. This intensifies the dissociation from their bodies and therefore from their selves. The following activities will help girls reconnect with their bodies:

Embodying Your Feelings

Everything we think, feel or do registers in our bodies through subtle changes in our musculature and in our bodily functions. Sometimes we can change how we feel just by changing how we hold our bodies. Have the girls:

> ➤ Walk around as if they have just won the lottery. Ask them to pay attention to how they hold their bodies.

> ➤ Walk around as if they are really depressed. What difference do they notice in how they hold their bodies?

> ➤ Imagine a situation where they are annoyed or angry with someone. Have them hunch their shoulders and say out loud "I am angry with you (name of person). Have them straighten up and pull their shoulders back and say the same thing. What kind of change has taken place? What kind of sensations do they experience in their body when they feel angry? Do they clench their jaw? Does their heart beat faster? What changes happen in their breathing?

> ➤ Remember a situation when they felt nervous or afraid. Ask the above questions.

Saying Yes! And Saying No!

This exercise allows girls to use their bodies to express their feelings. Girls love this exercise. The amount of female energy in the room is really powerful! On the count of three have girls:

> ➤ Clench their fists and jump up. As they come down have them yell "No!" as loud as they can. Repeat two more times.

> ➤ Jump up as high as they can and reach for the ceiling. As they come down, have them yell "Yes!" as loud as they can. Repeat two more times.

> ➤ Talk about why it is hard for some girls to say no and for others to say yes. What are the situations? What kind of support do they need?

Body Drawings

(You can do Part 1 or Part 2 separately, or both together.
You might have to do this activity over two sessions.)

Materials: roll of heavy brown or white paper / felt pens.

Part 1: Have girls draw an outline of each other's body. Have the girls use different color felt pens or crayons to color in these parts on the drawing of their own bodies:

➢ Those parts that they use a lot.

➢ Those parts that they really like.

➢ Those body parts that are the strongest, those that are the weakest.

➢ Those parts that they have confidence in—that work when they want them to.

➢ Those parts that give them pain.

➢ Those parts that make them feel embarrassed.

Part 2: Have the girls walk around as if they were alone in the room and as if:

➢ They were feeling angry. Where would they feel anger in their bodies?

➢ They were feeling sad. Where would they feel sadness in their bodies?

➢ They were feeling hurt. Where would they feel hurt in their bodies?

➢ They were feeling disappointed. Where would they feel disappointment in their bodies?

Using different colored felt pens, ask the girls to color in those places in their bodies where they feel those feelings. Remind them what it felt like when they walked around the room. If they don't know where the feeling is in their bodies, have them guess. Ensure the girls that there is no right or wrong to this activity.

NOTE: The *Breathing Exercises* on pages 116-117 are
another good way to help girls reconnect with their bodies.

COUNTERING THE POWER OF APPEARANCE

We all have moments when we wake up in the morning and stand before the mirror with our eyes shut, fervently hoping that when we open them the image of Cindy Crawford or Shania Twain will be looking back at us. When we open our eyes and Cindy or Shania are not there we have to find ways of feeling good about ourselves other than through how we look. Giving girls skills to counter the power of appearance is a key element of prevention to be integrated into our practice.

Why Different Girls Have Different Bodies

Girls come in all shapes and sizes. While society tells them they can change their body shape and type if they try hard enough, two things stand in the way—their metabolism and their genes. Providing girls with an understanding of why people have different bodies lessens the impact that the media has on them to conform to a specific size and shape. Understanding why some girls are fat and others are thin counters some of the weight prejudice that girls experience.

Understanding Metabolism...

We all need energy to survive. We obtain it by eating and by digesting food. The process of chemical digestion and its related reactions is called *metabolism*. Metabolism refers to the amount of energy or calories your body needs and burns to maintain itself. Whether you are eating, drinking, sleeping, talking to your friends or watching TV your body is constantly burning calories to keep you going. For some activities such as riding a bike your body needs to burn a lot of calories. For others, such as watching TV your body burns very few.

Imagine two different types of wood. One burns quickly when you set it on fire. The other one burns very slowly. You can burn more of the first kind of wood in the same amount of time that it takes to burn the second. The same is true of our bodies. Some bodies convert food into fuel and nutrients quickly and easily. Because these bodies have a 'fast' metabolism they use up a lot of calories and tend to be thin. Other bodies, however, are slower in converting food into fuel and nutrients and in burning off the energy or calories. They either need less calories/energy or store the energy they don't burn off. People with these bodies tend to be fat.

Metabolism is also affected by body composition or the amount of muscle you have compared to the amount of fat. Muscle uses more energy (calories) to maintain itself than fat so people who are more muscular and have a lower percentage of body fat are said to have a higher metabolism than others who are less muscular even though they might be the same height and weight.

Understanding Genes...

Every human is made up of billions of cells which are the tiny building blocks of our bodies. Each cell contains a substance called deoxyribonucleic acid or DNA for short. Long thin strands of DNA are wrapped together in the cell nucleus to form structures called chromosomes. Most cells in the body have 23 pairs of chromosomes, making a total of 46. One set of chromosomes comes from the mother through the egg and the other from the father through the sperm.

Genes are segments of or sections of DNA that are carried on the chromosomes and determine specific human characteristics such as eye and hair color. Most of the significant characteristics such as height, weight, blood group, skin color and intelligence are controlled by the combined actions of several genes. Because every person has about 30,000 different genes, the possibilities for individual differences in a specific trait increase when multiple genes are involved in regulating that trait. As a result although there might be strong similarities and tendencies between them, not all the children in one family look exactly alike or have all of the same traits or body types.

Different Body Types

Our bodies come in three body types (somatypes) that are genetically determined. They are based on the embryonic layers that each type is supposed to develop from. Endo means inside, as in the gut. Meso means muscle. Ecto refers to the outer layer—skin, for example, hence skinny. Although we tend towards one body type we all have characteristics of each in varying degrees.

Endomorph
  ➢ Tends towards carrying a lot of fat because body fat is stored easily.
  ➢ Some baseball catchers and pitchers, football players, weight lifters and golfers are endomorphs.

Mesomorph
  ➢ Tends towards muscularity with broad shoulders, narrow hips, large bones and heavy muscles – higher body weights.
  ➢ Many swimmers tend to be mesomorphs.

Ectomorph
  ➢ Tends towards being very lean with little muscle or fat.
  ➢ Long distance runners tend to be ectomorphs.

Most adolescents don't develop their natural body type until they are about 18 to 21 years old. Some people grow tall and bulk out later. Others bulk up first and grow taller later. Only 10% of the population are predominantly ectomorphs—yet the rest of us keep trying to make ourselves fit into this one type.

Body Connections and Heritage

We are all the product of our genetic heritage. We carry in our bodies our relationships with all the people in our lives, past and present. While we may not like all of the people we are related to, in acknowledging those body connections we reclaim our heritage. As girls try to conform to a specific and thus solitary body image they lose their connections to others and forget their heritage.

Celebrate Who You Are

Have girls bring in photographs of themselves. Have them write out what they feel to be their personal qualities inside themselves (e.g. creative, smart), and a description of themselves from the outside. Talk about what they can control and change and what remains the same. What different ways are there to celebrate who you are?

Look at Family Members

Bring in family pictures and discuss who girls resemble in their families. Have the girls tell stories about each of these people.

- ➤ Try to identify the predominant body type of each person. If both parents are large, girls have an 80% chance of being large. If one parent is large, girls have a 50% chance of being large. If someone looks like their Aunt Tessie and Aunt Tessie has big hips, their changes of looking like Tyra Banks are pretty slim (pardon the pun…).

- ➤ Look at how many different family members live in a girl's body—not only genetically but also in terms of the messages about their bodies that girls receive (and that they internalize) from family members. Encourage girls who are adopted to look at the traits of their adoptive families. How much do they resemble them and how are they different? Have them list the traits that they might pass on to their children.

Provide Role Models

Bring in pictures of girls and women of different body types. Magazines such as Radiance and New Moon feature a variety of body types and sizes. So do pictures of athletes. For example, look at a photograph of a woman's soccer or hockey team. Collect pictures of people from the newspaper. Hang the pictures in your classroom and in the halls of your school.

Create a Balanced Sense of Self

We can nurture *girlpower* by providing girls with other ways in which they can feel good about themselves in order to lessen the hold that appearance has on self-esteem and self worth and create a balance in their sense-of-self. This is an important, ongoing part of prevention that you can integrate into your daily practice.

➢ Help girls build a 'bank account' of self-esteem points. Give them specific feedback about their skills, qualities and talents. Tell them the things that you appreciate about them. Help them describe each other in the same way. Encourage girls to throw away empty descriptions such as' pretty' and 'nice'.

➢ Encourage girls to participate in activities that give them a sense of accomplishment. For some girls it may be participating in sports. For some it may be walking dogs at the local animal shelter and for some it may be volunteering in other ways.

➢ Help girls find a passion. The more girls focus on something that makes them feel good about themselves and gives them joy, the less likely they will focus on how they look.

➢ Encourage girls to name their heroes. Try to stay away from rock stars or movie stars. Talk about who these girls and women are and about their accomplishments. If girls could have lunch with these women, what would they want to ask them? What would they want to learn from them? What would they have to offer them? Choose a hero of the month and have the girls do research about her.

Creating Balance and Perspective

This exercise helps girls become aware of the emphasis they place on appearance.Give each girl a pie plate or have each girl draw a large circle on a piece of paper. Have the girls put a dot in the center.

➢ Have the girls divide the circle into six sections according to how important the following is to them. (You can change the categories or have them create the categories. Just make sure that one of those categories is appearance.)

• Appearance

• Family

• Friends

• School

• Hobbies or interests

• One area that they can choose.

➤ Have the girls talk about how they divided their circles.

- What is most important to them? Why?

- What area is least important to them? Why?

- What areas would they like to change? Why?

- What would they need to do to make that item less or more important?

- What stands in their way?

Note: This exercise is adapted from the Shape and Weight Based Self-esteem Inventory developed by J. Geller, C. Johnston and K. Madsen. Girls who have eating disorders or are at risk tend to place a lot of importance on appearance and therefore give it a large amount of space in their circle.

Sense-Of-Self Mobile

This exercise will help girls develop a balanced sense of themselves by helping them recognize qualities and characteristics other than how they look.

Materials (for each participant):

One 8¾" paper plate
Two index cards cut in quarters (8 pieces)
Eighteen paper clips

Eight pieces of string cut into 8" lengths
One 10" piece of string
Hole punch (optional)

Before starting the activity, punch 8 holes around the perimeter of the pie plate and one in the center. Punch a hole in each piece of index card (or pass around the hole punch to the girls).

Have the girls write one quality, characteristic, skill, role, interest or talent that she knows about herself on each card.

➤ Attach paper clips to both ends of the 8" pieces of string.

➤ Hook one end of the string into each card and the other into the edge pie plate.

➤ Attach paper clips to both ends of the 10" piece of string. Slip one paper clip through the hole in the center of the pie plate. Make sure the pie plate is upside down as it hangs better. Hang mobile.

You can also use this exercise to have the girls give each other feedback on the cards. Tell them that they cannot use words such as pretty and nice.

Adapted from Kathy J. Kater's *Healthy Body Image: Teaching Kids to Eat and Love their Bodies Too*
(Seattle: NEDA, 1998) Reprinted with permission of NEDA

Teach Girls How to Nourish Their Bodies

Many girls today are more concerned with being thin than with being healthy. They see food in terms of 'good' food and 'bad' food, 'healthy' food and 'junk' food. They cycle between not eating enough and then eating high fat, high calorie foods with their friends. They also monitor what their friends eat and reinforce a culture of dieting. The choices girls make in the food they eat are influenced by several factors:

Taste: Taste is the most important criteria. Foods that taste good make us feel good. Often, however it is the foods that are highest in fat that taste the best.

Family Behavior. Girls are more likely to eat breakfast if their parents do and are more likely to have a balance in their foods if the family eats to together.

Professionals and Volunteers: People who work with girls such as teachers, public health nurses, coaches, group facilitators and camp counselors can play an important role in encouraging girls to have balance in what they eat.

School Policies, Practices and Nutrition Education Programs: These work together to provide a key source of nutrition information, influence the availability of nutritious foods in the cafeteria, permit or ban vending machines in the school, provide food for students who otherwise would not have enough to eat and decide how much time students will have for lunch.

Media Messages: The media has a significant impact on food choices as it bombards girls with commercials about high fat, high calorie foods and at the same time reinforces the societal ideal of the thinness.

Peer Pressure: Girls practice and reinforce a culture of dieting. They watch each other and comment on what each other eats. They make comments such as "You're not going to eat that!!"

You can help girls make good choices by:

➤ Let girls know what different foods do and what happens when you don't eat enough—e.g. , you feel angry, irritable, fuzzy.

➤ Encourage girls to eat for energy by choosing food that tastes good and also helps their bodies perform. When girls diet they have no energy. They payoff of eating for energy is that they feel better in the long run.

➤ Encourage girls to eat whole foods which are low glycemic index carbohydrates such as fruits, vegetables, grains, whole wheat flour and brown rice. Glycemic index is the rate at which the body breaks down carbohydrates into glucose— the sugar that is the body's fuel. Foods with a low glycemic index are broken down more slowly than foods with a high glycemic index and can help stabilize blood sugar and mood. Have girls monitor how they feel when they eat this way over a period of time.

➢ Have girls include enough milk products to satisfy their calcium requirements in order to build strong bones.

➢ Let girls know that their bodies need some fat. Encourage them to include healthy oils from fish, nuts, seeds, vegetable oils and soy foods.

➢ Encourage girls to eat breakfast so that they can have the energy they need to do their daily activities. Skipping breakfast makes them feel 'fuzzy' and often means they will overeat later on.

➢ Encourage girls to cut down on caffeine. Many girls consume several cups of coffee a day including lattes as well as the equivalent of three to five cups of coffee a day in caffeinated sodas.

➢ Place the emphasis on balance. Eating for energy does not mean eating low calorie or diet foods. It also doesn't mean depriving yourself of chocolate, burgers or pizza. When girls do eat fast food, encourage them to limit the servings they receive. Many restaurants today offer more fries and bigger drinks for just a little bit more money. It's always hard to resist a bargain.

➢ Encourage your school to serve nutritious meals in the cafeteria and to limit high fat/high sugar snacks in vending machines. Many school cafeterias feature fast food while rejecting foods high in calcium such as milk and yogurt.

Sources:

Ann Douglas & Julie Douglas. *Body Talk: The Straight Facts on Fitness, Nutrition & Feeling Great About Yourself.* Toronto: Maple Tree Press, 2002

Sandra Susan Friedman. *When Girls Feel Fat: Helping Girls Through Adolescence.* Toronto: HarperCollins, 1997, 2000

J. Geller, C. Johnston & K. Madsen. "A new measure of the role of shape and weight in self-concept: The Shape and Weight Based Self-Esteem Inventory." *Cognitive Therapy and Research,* 21, 5-24. 1997

Kathy J. Kater. *Healthy Body Image: Teaching Kids to Eat and Love their Bodies Too.* Seattle: NEDA, 1998

Linda Omichinski. *Hugs For Teens & Diets: No Weigh - Building the road to healthier living.* VI Parents' Guide, HUGS International Inc, 1995

TeensHealth, "The Basics on Genes and Genetic Disorders," www.teenshealth.org

DIETING MYTHS

Risk Factors Addressed:
Dieting
Parents Who Model and Stress Thinness
Body Dissatisfaction

Most of us have been on diets. We usually go on one during the stressful periods in our lives. When we feel we can't control what goes on in our lives, we try to control our food. Every time we start a diet we know this diet is going to be *the* diet—the one that finally works. We count the pounds we are going to lose and envision ourselves in the dress that is now one size too small and has been hanging in our closet forever. We imagine ourselves doing all of the things that we have put off until we lose that weight.

There is such a feeling of cleansing and purity that goes with beginning the diet. We throw out all the bad food and replace it with whatever good food is required by the current diet that this time will change our lives. For the first few days (even weeks) we feel in control. We sometimes even feel righteous. Look at all those other people eating pizza and ice cream! Look at how healthy we will be!

Alas, there comes a time in every diet when we begin to feel the effects of the deprivation. When that happens, we eat as if our grocery store or supermarket is going to go out of business along with all the others in a 200-mile radius. I remember my surprise during my dieting years when I found out ice cream had an expiry date. I couldn't imagine anyone having ice cream long enough to let it get stale. When we finish eating we feel guilty. After a while, however, we recover and we begin the next diet that is going to be the diet that will change our lives forever.

As adults we pass the dieting torch on to our girls. We do this when we make comments about girls' bodies or about our own, and when we practice fat prejudice. We do this when as parents we insist our daughters reflect well upon us with an acceptable body size and shape and when we encourage girls to lose weight to fit in with their friends. We do this as coaches when we convince girls that being thinner will help them swim and run faster, do a higher triple lutz or gain a position on the soccer team.

Most little girls who begin to diet have not yet integrated beliefs about dieting and thinness with beliefs about attractiveness. They are dieting because that's what they see their mother doing and because they are learning to respond to the cultural norms as every woman does. During adolescence, peer groups reinforce the importance of thinness with fat talk (grungies) and the need to engage in weight-loss behaviors. The rejection of fatness becomes a shared value in the group. Talking about dieting not only serves as a means of giving and receiving information about weight control but is also a means of reinforcing the cultural obsession with weight and the prejudice towards fat.

Disordered eating practices are so common that in order to fit in, girls have to be preoccupied with losing weight even when they feel good about their bodies. If you want to know what a particular girl is doing to manage her weight all you have to do is look at her friends' attitudes towards their bodies and their weight management practices and dieting behaviors.

Did You Know?

➤ Girls begin to restrict their food intake when they are as young as five.
(Feldman, Feldman & Goodmanl, 1986)

➤ Forty-five percent of children in grades 3 to 6 want to be thinner.
(Maloney, McGuire, Daniels & Specker, 1990)

➤ As girls go through puberty, 14% of 11 to 12 year old girls have significant concerns about weight and shape. (Cooper & Goodyer, 1997)

➤ Eighty per cent of girls of normal height and weight want to lose weight.
(Berg, 1992)

➤ Up to 35% of normal dieters will head down the continuum of disordered eating into full-blown eating disorders. (Shisslak,. Grago & Estes, 1995)

When Girls Diet

When girls first go on diets it is a positive experience for them. Their friends compliment them on their weight loss. For a short period of time they feel a sense of accomplishment which allows them to feel good about themselves. Some girls feel a sense of superiority because they can control their hunger while others around them can't. Soon, however, this sense of control disappears because it is illusionary. In order to recapture it girls up the ante ——they restrict their food intake even more. As they get caught in the psychological dynamics of dieting and restriction they begin the trek down the road to anorexia. For some girls the dieting bubble bursts when the effects of deprivation set in. These girls overcompensate for not eating enough by eating too much. They binge eat and purge which puts them at risk of bulimia or begin a cycle of weight loss and regain which puts them at risk of high blood pressure and cardiovascular disease.

The Effects of Dieting

The effects of dieting are far reaching. Set point' theory suggests that diets do not work as we suppose and can, in fact, make us fat! The 'set point' theory holds that everyone has a genetically determined weight range our body attempts to maintain. When we diet our body cannot tell the difference between a deliberately constructed low-calorie diet where we are deliberately not eating enough and an actual famine. It seeks to protect itself from starvation by burning calories much more slowly, thus needing less to maintain itself. When we go off the diet, our body works not only to regain the weight that we have lost, but also to store extra in the event that we try to starve it again. The set point is thus raised to a higher natural weight range and we eventually gain additional poundage.

Let's say that we lose 50 pounds just by dieting. A good part of these pounds will be muscle. When we go off the diet—and 97% of us eventually do—our body composition changes. The weight we gain back is not composed of the muscle we lost but of fat which requires less calories so our metabolism is now a lot slower in converting food into energy than it was before. Because our fat storage enzymes become more efficient at their job—an evolutionary strategy to keep us alive during times of famine—we gain weight on the same amount or even fewer calories than we were eating before we started dieting.

Dieting may interfere with normal growth and development in children and adolescents. Dieting can make them depressed and dizzy and can decrease their concentration and even rob them of IQ points. Despite the fact diets don't work we still keep following the dream of achieving the ideal body. Dieting is the most potent political sedative in women's history. It creates passivity, low self-esteem and anxiety and ensures that we remain focused on our weight instead of on our lives, on changing our natural bodies instead of creating social change.

Getting Girls Off Diets and Keeping Them Off

> Provide information: use the information in this chapter as well as the information on different bodies in the previous chapter and in the section on media on page 99.

> Teach skills: reread *Practicing Assertive Behavior* on page 64 and *Yes, but...* on page 67 as well as the section on bullying and teasing. Use the exercises to role-play situations where girls are pressured by their friends to diet and how they can respond. Remember to support girls when they do stand up to their friends.

> Be a role model: get off your own diet. Share your struggles with girls when it seems appropriate.

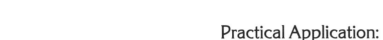

Practical Application:

Have the girls take the True or False test *EXPLORING THE MYTHS ABOUT DIETING* on page 86 and discuss their answers. You can use this test with the girls that you work with in both Prevention and Intervention.

Answers:

1 – False	4 – False	7 – False	10 – True	13 – True
2 – True	5 – False	8 – True	11 – False	14 – True
3 – False	6 – False	9 – True	12 – False	

WHAT REALLY HAPPENS WHEN WE DIET page 87 provides you and the girls with practical information about dieting.

TOP TEN REASONS TO GIVE UP DIETING

#10: Diets don't work. Even if you lose weight, you will probably gain it all back and you might gain back more.

#9: Diets are expensive. If you did not buy special diet products, you could save enough to get new clothes, which would improve your outlook right now.

#8: Diets are boring. People on diets talk and think about food and practically nothing else. There's a lot more to life.

#7: Diets don't necessarily improve your health. Like the weight loss, health improvement is temporary. Dieting can actually cause health problems.

#6: Diets don't make you beautiful. Very few people will ever look like models. Glamour is a look, not a size. You don't have to be thin to be attractive.

#5: Diets are not sexy. If you want to feel and be more attractive, take care of your body and your appearance. Feeling healthy makes you look your best.

#4. Diets can turn into eating disorders. The obsession to be thin can lead to anorexia, bulimia bingeing and compulsive exercise.

#3. Diets can make you afraid of food. Food nourishes and comforts us, and gives us pleasure. Dieting can make food seem like your enemy, and can deprive you of all the positive things about food.

#2. Diets can rob you of energy. If you want to lead a full and active life, you need good nutrition, and enough food to meet your body's needs.

#1. Learning to love and accept yourself just as you are will give you self-confidence, better health and a sense of well-being that will last a lifetime.

EXPLORING THE MYTHS ABOUT DIETING*

True or False?

Read each statement and check the box that you think is correct:

True?	False?	
		1. Dieting always leads to permanent weight loss.
		2. Each person has their own natural weight.
		3. It's easy to lose weight!
		4. All fat people are fat because they overeat.
		5. All fat people are unhealthy.
		6. Thin people are healthier than fat people.
		7. Eating normally means eating only diet foods.
		8. Dieting may cause weight gain.
		9. Most diets don't work.
		10. Normal eating means eating a variety of foods.
		11. It's easy for everyone to gain weight.
		12. Everyone can change their body type.
		13. Dieting can lead to an eating disorder.
		14. Dieting can make a person unhealthy.

*Adapted from *Teacher's Resource Kit*
National Eating Disorder Information Centre, Toronto, Ontario, Canada

WHAT *REALLY* HAPPENS WHEN WE DIET*

HOW WE DIET	THIS IS WHAT *REALLY* HAPPENS
Skipping meals or decreasing calories	√ This lowers metabolism so we store fat more easily from fewer calories. √ The brain's and muscle's demand for fuel causes rebound "munchies," usually for high fat and high sugar items. √ Poor attention span, irritability, fatigue. √ Muscle tissue may be lost.
Cut out carbohydrates	√ Your body loses its best source of stable energy. You'll be more likely to feel moody and tired. √ You'll end up eating higher fat and sugary foods to satisfy munchies.
Cut out meats without comparable replacement	√ May risk iron deficiency which leads to fatigue. √ Energy from meals may not last as long, causing more hunger between meals for high fat, high sugar foods.
Go on preplanned meal replacement diet or liquid diet	√ You have a 95% chance of regaining any weight you lose in 1 to 3 years. √ You give away control to the plan, which lowers your self-esteem. √ You often lose muscle mass along with fat. This lowers your metabolism, making it easier to store fat on fewer calories. √ Habits are replaced temporarily, not changed permanently. Also, it's expensive.
Fasting	√ Most of the weight lost is water. √ Muscle mass decreases—which lowers metabolism. Subsequent fat gain. √ Can be medically dangerous for some individuals.

WHY WE DIET	THIS IS WHAT *REALLY* HAPPENS
To be slim	√ Slimness is temporary. Over the long run, 95% of dieters regain the weight. Many women get fatter, so they diet again, with similar poor results. This is called yo yo dieting and it can lead to obesity.
To be healthier	√ *Yo Yo dieting* increases health risks more than being fat. √ There is no evidence that fat in itself is unhealthy. It is inactivity and too much high fat high caloric food which puts people at risk. There *is* evidence to show that being too thin is unhealthy. √ Most dieting decreases our muscle mass. Muscles are needed for good health. √ Many diets are unhealthy. Your body and mind don't run well when you restrict calories. Dieting makes you moody and irritable, and makes you obsessed with food. This feels like failure, but in fact it is a physiological response and has nothing to do with will power.
To be more attractive	√ What attracts you to someone else? Do you want your friends to like you for your body or yourself? What are long term relationships based upon? If you are dieting, are you any fun to be around?

*Adapted from material developed by Cathy Richards
for the British Columbia Interior Health Region.

PHYSICAL ACTIVITY

Risk Factors Addressed:
Body Dissatisfaction
Self Esteem
Being Fat

Physical activity is a major component in the prevention of eating disorders and in addressing obesity. Girls who participate in physical activity on a regular basis are better able to remain connected to their bodies during adolescence. They are more able to experience them kinesthetically from the inside instead of focusing on how their different body parts look from the outside. Physical activity helps girls and young women take charge of their bodies by making them aware of their physical capacity and by providing them with a sense of ownership. Girls learn how to listen to their own bodies for signs of fatigue, overexertion and pain. Being active allows girls to enjoy their own physical natures—to experience their bodies as expansive, joyful and sensuous. By experiencing their bodies as functional rather than decorative, girls are more likely to feel positive about them regardless of their size.

Many other health and social benefits derive from being physically active. Girls who participate in 30 minutes of regular physical activity benefit from improved health, fitness and motor skills and have increased aerobic capacity, strength and endurance. Physical activity can buffer the effects of anxiety and depression. It has a positive effect on how girls do in school in terms of memory, observation and problem solving ability, as well as in significant improvements in attitudes, discipline, behaviors and creativity. Adolescent girls who participate in sports are less likely to engage in sex at a younger age, and if they are sexually active, are less likely to have unprotected sex. They are also less likely to smoke or get involved with drugs.

Group activities and team sports offer girls the chance to make friends and develop meaningful relationships with peers and caring adults. They learn teamwork, cooperation, sharing and working towards a common goal—values that not only help girls in their personal and social lives but also later on, when they enter the work world.

Physical Activity is Both a Protective Factor and a Risk Factor

While physical activity is a valuable and powerful protective factor, it can also be a risk factor in the development of an eating disorder. When we make weight loss/control the goal of physical activity self-esteem becomes dependent on the bathroom scale instead of being a by product of being physically active and strong. We also shame girls who are fat or who see themselves as fat and place them at risk of dieting.

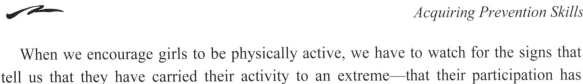

When we encourage girls to be physically active, we have to watch for the signs that tell us that they have carried their activity to an extreme—that their participation has moved from fun, enjoyment and challenge to obsession, performance and perfection. Pages 19-20 address how to recognize and deal with girls who are caught up in compulsive exercise.

Encourage Girls to Use Their Bodies

Once girls reach grade seven their aerobic fitness level begins to decline. Keep in mind how self-conscious girls can be about their bodies once they reach puberty. Many girls try to avoid PE because they don't want to undress in front of other girls. They wear tee shirts over their bathing suits when they go swimming. Many girls have not learned to perform basic bodily movements with confidence and many have not had the chance to develop skills such as throwing, catching and hitting. Even when girls are given the opportunity they may not participate because their skill level is low, they are afraid they will be teased if they are fat and because they are afraid they will fail.

> ➤ Encourage girls to use their bodies to feel strong. Introduce them to a range of activities and help them find the ones that feel good to them. Some bodies are built for short-term speed, some for endurance. Focus on enjoyment, participation and skill development. It is important to continuously stress that thin does not mean fit, you can be fat and still be fit.

> ➤ Integrate opportunities to be active into your classroom, your group and your life. It can be as little as snacking on exercise for 10 minutes three times a day to planning longer games and activities.

> ➤ Make it normative that bodies need to move and get stimulation. When girls get fidgety let them know that their bodies have a "hunger to move."

> ➤ Encourage girls-only opportunities for skill development and safe play. Make sure girls receive the same amount of gym time and playground space that boys do.

> ➤ Encourage all parents, teachers and administrators to support girls in physical activities. There is power in numbers.

> ➤ Provide alternative and modified physical activities for girls who are disabled.

> ➤ Provide activities and opportunities for girls of different body types. E.g., girls who are runners may not have the same body type as girls who enjoy hiking or swimming.

> ➤ Check out my book BODY THIEVES. The book will give you an understanding of and context for many of the issues around physical activity and sport as well as skills and strategies to get girls active.

WHEN GIRLS *ARE* FAT

Risk Factors Addressed:
Body Dissatisfaction
Self Esteem
Being Fat

Despite our societal obsession with thinness and the billions of dollars that people spend to lose weight, the average person is fatter today than at any time in history. From 1991 to 1999 the prevalence of obesity increased by 57% in adults.[1] From 1981 to 1996 the prevalence of being overweight increased by 92% in boys and 57% in girls.[2] The rate of obesity among boys aged seven to thirteen nearly tripled from 5% to 13.5% over this period of time while the prevalence of obesity among girls of the same age more than doubled to 11.8%.[3] Today the prevalence of childhood obesity in Canada and the United States are the same—double that of European countries such as England, Scotland and Spain.

The Crisis of Childhood Obesity

Obesity is the medical term for the degree of fatness at the far end of the continuum of weight. It is generally regarded as a body weight of 20% or more than what is considered 'ideal' or 'normal'. It is measured by the Body Mass Index (BMI) which keeps changing its parameters over time and therefore changes the definition of 'normal' according to current beliefs and myths around fat. The BMI does not take into account racial differences in people, body composition such as muscle/fat ratio, nor the general health of the person, and it varies considerably with age in growing children—particularly girls.

While very fat children are at a higher risk of developing juvenile diabetes and may develop other health problems later in life, it is not fat itself that is the issue but rather the decrease in physical activity and the increase in the amount of high-fat nutritionally empty foods that children eat. When we try to eliminate or reduce fat by dieting we create a cure that is far worse than the disease. And while we may recognize the potential health risks associated with childhood obesity we tend to overlook the equally harmful social and psychological consequences of being fat in a society where there is a strong cultural prejudice against fat people and an obsession with being thin.

[1] A.H. Mokdad, M.K. Sedrula, W.H. Dietz, B.A. Bowman, J.S. Marks, & J.P. Koplan. "The continuing epidemic of obesity in the United States." *JAMA*, 284: 1650 – 1, 2000

[2] R. E. Anderson. "The spread of the childhood obesity epidemic." *Canadian Medical Association Journal*, 163(11): 1461-1462, 2000

[3] M. S. Tremblay and D. Willms. "Secular trends in the body mass index of Canadian children." *Canadian Medical Association Journal,* 163(11): 1429-1433, 2000

Fat Prejudice

It is difficult to be a fat girl or boy. Weight prejudice is one of the few socially accepted forms of prejudice and discrimination remaining in our society. While it may no longer be acceptable to make comments about someone's race, religion, gender or sexual orientation, it seems perfectly acceptable to make hurtful comments about their weight. Fat people are seen as weak, lazy, sloppy, incompetent and lacking self-control. Despite evidence to the contrary, society still promotes the belief that people can change their size and shape if they try hard enough, that inside every fat person is a thin person struggling to get out—because it goes without saying that everyone wants to be thin.

Did You Know?

➢ Young girls are more afraid of becoming fat that they are of nuclear war, cancer, or losing their parents. (The Council on Size and Weight Discrimination)

➢ Over half of the females between the ages of 18 and 25 would prefer to be run over by a truck than be fat. (Gaesser, 1996)

➢ Eleven percent of parents would abort a fetus that was genetically coded to be overweight. (Fraser, 1997)

➢ Children who are obese rate their quality of life as low as that of young patients on chemotherapy. (JAMA, 2003)

Society's prejudice towards fat is internalized by girls and boys at an early age and becomes entrenched as they grow up. When pre-school children are given the opportunity to play with dolls, all children—even those who could correctly identify that the fat dolls looked more like them—prefer to play with the thin dolls. Nursery school children rate figure drawings of fat children more negatively than drawings of children with physical disabilities. When shown silhouettes of fat and thin males and females, nine-year-old children rate the fat figures as having significantly fewer friends, being less liked by their parents, doing less well at school, being less content with their appearance and wanting to be thinner.

Children who are fat are teased about their size and may have trouble playing certain sports or avoid physical activity altogether because they are self-conscious of their bodies. Prejudice towards fat robs them of their self-esteem. It makes it difficult for them to feel loved and accepted in a society that rejects them because it finds their size unacceptable. Their low self-esteem and hatred of their bodies is often caused not by being fat but by the shame that they are made to experience in a culture that only values people who are thin.

EXPLORING OUR BELIEFS ABOUT FAT

Indicate whether you think the statement is
true (T) or false (F) for each of the following:

_____1. Fat people eat more than thin people.

_____2. A slow metabolism is just an excuse for being fat.

_____3. Fat people are not as competent as thin people.

_____4. You can change your body type if you try hard enough.

_____5. Being female means having a certain amount of fat on your body.

_____6. Only thin people are fit.

_____7. Heredity has a lot to do with being fat.

_____8. Inside every fat person is a thin person who is trying to get out.

_____9. Anyone can become and remain thin through a "sensible" diet.

_____10. When people lose weight we should compliment them.

_____11. Everybody should lose weight for health reasons.

_____12. We should help girls lose weight so that they can fit in with their peers.

_____13. It's important to weigh ourselves every day so that we can keep our weight under control.

_____14. Our dieting behavior has an effect on girls.

_____15. We should encourage fat girls to develop their personality.

_____16. We should not accept fat girls as they are because this encourages them to stay fat instead of doing something about it.

EXPLORING OUR BELIEFS ABOUT FAT

Take the test, *Exploring Our Beliefs About Fat*. Explore your own beliefs about fat, and separate what is myth from what is true. You can use this quiz and/or adapt it in your work with girls. It's a good way of fighting fat prejudice.

1. **Fat people eat more than thin people.**

   False: Twelve out of thirteen studies reviewed in *The Energy Balance and Obesity in Man* by J.S. Garrow (NY: American Elsevier, 1974) found the intake of fat people equal to or less than that of thin people.

2. **A slow metabolism is just an excuse for being fat.**

   False: People have different metabolisms. Basal metabolism—the minimum amount of energy needed to carry on vital body processes—is affected by age, size, body composition (muscle: fat ratios), gender, genetics and life stage. Yet even when people are matched for these characteristics, their metabolism varies.

3. **Fat people are not as competent as thin people.**

   False: If we believed this, we would choose a surgeon by the size of her thighs.

4. **You can change your body type if you try hard enough.**

   False: A person's type is determined by a number of factors including genetics.

5. **Being female means having a certain amount of fat on your body.**

   True: Fat is necessary for menstruation and therefore for conception. It aids in the production of the hormone estrogen.

6. **Only thin people are fit.**

   False: Many thin people are not fit because they do not use their bodies. Many fat people exercise and are strong and fit regardless of their weight.

7. **Heredity has a lot to do with being fat.**

   True: According to Toronto General Hospital, heredity is responsible for 81% of differences in body size.

8. **Inside every fat person is a thin person trying to get out.**

   False: This makes the assumption that everyone wants to and should be thin. It teaches people that being fat is bad and unacceptable.

9. **Anyone can become thin and remain thin through a 'sensible' diet.**

   False: 95% of people who diet regain the weight they lost. They often gain additional weight within two or three years. Differences in our metabolism mean that not everybody is capable of becoming and remaining thin. Many people who are fat especially those who have become fat through yo-yo dieting will likely remain so.

10. **When people lose weight we should compliment them.**

False: If you tell people how great they look because they lost weight, what do you tell them when they gain the weight back? Complimenting someone on their weight loss perpetuates the myths being thin is intrinsically good and everyone wants to and can be thin. It also puts a lot of pressure on them to maintain the weight loss when statistically they have a very good chance of regaining it—plus more.

11. **Everybody should lose weight for health reasons.**

False: While there are health risks associated with being fat, there are also some health benefits. It may be healthier to remain at a stable high weight than to yo yo diet. Given that permanent weight loss is elusive for most fat people, the only true option to them is to be as healthy as they can regardless of their weight.

12. **We should help girls lose weight so that they can fit in with their peers.**

False: Encouraging girls to diet so that they can fit in with their peers perpetuates the idea we can judge a girl by her appearance. It also is dangerous. Some girls carry it to the extreme. Others become chronic dieters. Because of their genetics and metabolism some girls cannot keep the weight off regardless of how much we help them.

13. **It is important to weigh ourselves everyday so that we can keep our weight under control.**

False: Frequent weighing reinforces the obsession with food and weight. The only ones who should have scales are grocers and fish.

14. **Our dieting behavior has an effect on girls.**

True: A recent study of 8 year old children (86 girls and 90 boys) found that girls are aware of dieting and are drawn to weight control as a means of improving self-worth and that their mothers are influential in this regard. (A.J. Hill and V. Pallin, "Dieting Awareness and Low Self-Worth: Related Issues in 8 Year Old Girls." International Journal of Eating Disorders, December 1998: 24(4): 405-413)

15. **We should encourage fat girls to develop their personalities in order to be accepted.**

False: We should encourage all girls to develop their personalities regardless of appearance. Encouraging only fat girls to do so in order to be accepted tells them that they are not beautiful the way that they are.

16. **We should not accept fat girls as they are because this encourages them to stay fat instead of doing something about it.**

False: Girls are fat for many reasons. Bullying them into becoming thin just makes them feel badly about themselves and increases their stress of being fat in a thin world. The more criticized and unsafe girls feel, the less likely they will try to make changes in their lifestyle.

WHY GIRLS MAY BE FAT

Our body weight is the result of a complex mix of biological, social, environmental and psychological issues as well as lifestyle practices. Girls may be fat because of…

Genetics:

As pages 75-76 described, genes and metabolism play a major part in determining our body type and weight. Even though there is an unhealthy emphasis on thinness today, there was a time when fat was necessary for survival—this is still the case in many third world countries where there is not enough food. Your fat genes might be your legacy from your loving grandmother and/or your grouchy Uncle Al.

Emotional Eating:

When girls gain weight rapidly (especially when they are young) it is often a sign that something is not right in their lives. Pages 12-13 describe how girls use food as a coping mechanism to deal with scary situations and feelings and with stressors in their lives. Emotional eating may also signal depression—something we need to pay attention to.

Faulty Hunger Mechanisms:

Because children are 'wired' differently some can eat until they are full and some don't ever know when to stop. Faulty hunger mechanisms may also be the result of restriction. When parents unwisely restrict the amount of food that they give their children, the children compensate by overeating. Just like dieters, these children damage their hunger mechanism and lose the ability to know when they are hungry and when they are full. They also become preoccupied with food.

The Food We Eat:

There was a time when we prepared food from scratch and created a balance in the kind of foods that we ate. Because of the lack of time in our lives convenience foods that are high in fat and in calories often make up the major part of what we eat. As well, because the fast food industry markets 'super size' portions, children see this as 'normal' and eat twice as much as their bodies need. Many schools are top heavy on fries and low on fruits, vegetables and yogourt. In many schools soft drink and snack vending machines earn money to make up for the shortfalls from budget cuts. Often children only have 15 minutes to eat.

Poverty:

For many people balanced eating is a luxury. It costs a lot less to serve your family Kraft Dinner every day than to include fresh fruits and vegetables as a regular part of their meals.

Lack of Physical Activity:

Children lead increasingly sedentary lives. They no longer play outside because there is no one to look out for them. Often they are driven to school, the mall and to their activities. Watching television not only encourages inactivity but also snacking. The more television kids watch, the more likely it is they will gain weight over time. Many schools have cut back on their physical education programs—despite recommendations that children should participate in 30 minutes of physical activity a day. Many parents just don't have time or the opportunity to be physically active with their kids.

Dieting and Binge Eating:

Girls are beginning to diet at younger and younger ages. Dieting causes them to become obsessed with food and to engage in dysfunctional eating. While dieting is a prime risk factor for developing an eating disorder, yo-yo dieting (chronic dieting interspersed with overeating) makes them fatter.

PROMOTING SIZE ACCEPTANCE

Prevention is about size acceptance and about being fit and healthy at whatever size we are. We need to value girls and boys of all shapes and sizes—including those who are fat. Until we can reduce fat to just a description of size and not a description of character and until we can make it acceptable for people to be fat we will continue to see an increase in eating disorders and childhood obesity no matter how hard we try to prevent them.

Fat is Just a Three-Letter Word

In my professional training workshops there are always participants who have difficulty with the concept of size acceptance. While they may agree we should accept girls of all shapes and sizes, that acceptance often stops when girls are even a teeny bit 'overweight.' Even though they can accept that dieting is dangerous and doesn't work and can make you sick and is a risk factor for eating disorders, none of this seems to apply when we talk about fat girls.

> There is a fundamental paradox in our professional and societal beliefs and attitudes about dieting: what is diagnosed as *disordered eating* in thin people is prescribed for fat people.
>
> Patricia Lyons, 2000

It is very difficult for many of us—especially those of us who are members of the health profession—to get beyond the belief that anyone can and should maintain a 'healthy weight' through 'healthy eating' and a 'healthy lifestyle.' Our attitudes towards fat are often punitive: if a girl is fat it must be her fault or her parents' fault. We are afraid that if we accept someone who is even a little bit fat, we are condoning something we are told over and over again is bad. We can't see that people can, in fact, participate in healthy eating and have a healthy lifestyle and still be fat.

While weight loss may be beneficial to some people, the strong link between self-worth and body size in our society often sets in motion the yo-yo dieting/eating disorder cycle and intensifies the preoccupation with appearance. As well, it is difficult to focus on weight loss without making people feel badly about themselves.

If dieting didn't exist and wasn't an option we would help girls be fat with dignity. We would encourage them to be physically active so that they could be healthy. Once they began to feel strong in their bodies and good about themselves we could encourage them to eat for energy and introduce balance in what they eat. We would support them and their families in making these changes. Ironically, in such a world girls might lose weight from these changes in their lifestyle. Then again, they might not. What's important is the goal of our intervention would be nurturing *girlpower* not making girls thin. When the goal is weight loss we only reinforce the low self-esteem that fat girls already feel and start them on a cycle that will inevitably make them fail and/or make them sick.

NURTURING girlpower WHEN GIRLS *ARE* FAT

➤ Help her be fat with dignity. We all need to be proud of who we are. Many adults put their futures on hold—waiting until they lose weight for their 'life' to begin. Let's not do this to our girls!

➤ Listen to her feelings about being different without trying to fix things. When we try to 'protect' girls from hurt by ignoring their fat, we pretend that something that is a major issue in their lives doesn't exist.

➤ Teach her (and all children) about genetics and metabolism. This lets them know it is normal for them to come in all sizes and shapes and there is no 'fault' attached to being fat.

> Let her know fat is a body type and not a character type. Diffuse the value judgments around fat by using the word in the same way that you use the words for other physical characteristics.

> Let her know she is beautiful. There is more than one narrow definition of beauty in the world even though so many people attempt to ascribe to it.

> Don't tell her that it's 'what's inside that counts' and that she should develop her personality. This is true for children of all sizes and shapes, not just for those who are fat. It also makes it sound like personality is some kind of consolation prize.

> Introduce her (and all family members and students) to a range of foods and encourage them to create balance and to eat for energy. Healthy eating does not mean eating only diet foods even though that is the definition we tend to give it.

> Bring in pictures of girls and women of a whole range of body sizes and talk about them in terms other than of how they look. Take pictures of active people of all shapes and sizes.

> Encourage her (and all other girls) to use her body so she can be proud of her strength.

> Help her deal with teasing and bullying.

> Lobby for zero tolerance for bullying in your school.

> Become a *Size Acceptance Warrior* and fight fat prejudice.

Sources:

F. Berg. "Who is dieting in the United States?" *Healthy Weight Journal*, pp. 48-49, May/June 1992

F. Berg. "Integrated approach: Health at any size," *Healthy Weight Journal*, p. 74, September/October 1999

P. J. Cooper & I. Goodyer. "Prevalence and significance of weight and shape concerns in girls aged 11-16 years old," *British Journal of Psychiatry*, 171:542-544, Dec: 1997

W.F Feldman, E. Feldman & J. Goodman. "Health concerns and health related behaviors of adolescents," *CMAJ*, No. 134: 489-493, 1986

N. Goodman, S.A. Richardson, S.M.Dornbush and A.H. Hastorf. "Variant reactions to physical disabilities," *American Sociological Review*, 28: 429-435, 1963

Hill & Silver (1995) in M. I. Loewy "Working with fat children in schools," *Radiance Magazine*, Fall: 1998

P. Lyons. "Fat and fit: An idea whose time has come," *Melpomene*, Vol. 15, No. 3, Fall: 1996

M.J. Maloney, J. McGuire, S.R. Daniels & B. Specker. "Dieting behavior and eating attitudes in children," *Pediatrics*, 85(5): 714, May: 1990

E.D Rothblum. "The stigma of women's weight: Social and economic realities," *Feminism and Psychology*, 2: 61-73, 1992

Catherine M. Shisslak, Marjorie Crago, Linda S. Estes & Norma Gray. "Content and Method of Developmentally Appropriate Prevention Programs," in Linda Smolak, Michael P. Levine & Ruth Streigel-Moore, eds. *The Developmental Psychopathology of Eating Disorders*. New Jersey: Lawrence Erlbaum Associates, 1996

MEDIA

Risk Factors Addressed:
  Body Dissatisfaction
  Social Comparison
  High exposure to unhealthy and
    unrealistically thin body image ideals
  Low Self-Esteem

It's almost impossible to escape the pervasive influence of the media. Children watch an average of four hours of television every day. By the time they reach high school they have watched approximately 15,000 hours of TV compared to the 11,000 hours they have spent in school. Electronic media shape the way children are reared and socialized and the way they learn to manage their lives. By selecting and manipulating reality the media defines and reflects what is normal, acceptable and ideal, and emphasizes and reinforces the values and images of those who create the advertising messages and own the means by which these messages are disseminated. Where in the past stories were told by parents or others in the community who were connected to the child (and related in the context of the child's life), the stories children hear today are told by disconnected and distant corporate conglomerates that have something to sell.

When children watch television programs and rock videos, play computer games and listen to music they have a passive relationship to the media. They take in copious amounts of material (images and messages) without ever discussing what they see. Children don't have the cognitive skills, critical capacity or life experience to evaluate the credibility of this information. They tend to believe most of what they see is real. They cannot distinguish between fantasy and reality, to understand irony or disregard stereotypes.

For most children brand awareness begins in the crib. At six months, just as they are beginning to mouth simple sounds like 'da da' they are also forming mental images of corporate logos. One in four children now utters a brand name as her first recognizable word. By the time they are two children are asking for products by brand name. Not only is television viewing on the rise among preschoolers but so is aggressive marketing to toddlers.

The Media and Gender Stereotypes

The media is quite rigid in its gender stereotypes. Women and girls are more likely to be shown in the home joyfully performing domestic chores such as cooking, cleaning and laundry. Men, including Mr. Clean, rarely get their hands dirty unless they are removing grease from such manly places such as the garage. Women are still portrayed as sex objects in order to sell products, or as victims who can't protect themselves and are the natural recipients of beatings, harassment, sexual assault and murder. Women who have careers are usually portrayed as young and thin—leaving the impression a degree in medicine comes from Jenny Craig. By the time women reach the age of 30, they begin to disappear from major roles. Nine out of ten women who appear on TV are under the age of 46. Women age faster than men and as they age they are portrayed as sexless and more sinister and evil.

Masculinity is often associated with machismo, independence, competition, emotional detachment, aggression and violence. A real man drives his car at full speed and his SUV into environmentally sensitive areas. In prime-time television men outnumber women two to one. When both men and women reach 60, they begin to disappear altogether. Low income wage earners of both sexes are virtually invisible. There has been a decline in the number of characters with disabilities, and mentally-ill characters and 'foreigners' fail most often at what they do and commit most crime and violence.

Children who live without television have fewer gender biases. Once exposed to TV, their attitudes and beliefs change. The more television children watch, the more likely they are to hold sexist notions about traditional male and female roles and the more likely the boys are to demonstrate aggressive behavior.

An Altered Picture of Perfection

As girls make the transition into adolescence, the media usher them psychologically into a culture based upon and reinforcing unattainable 'perfection.' Because girls rarely see photos of full-bodied, fat or average sized girls and women, they come to believe abnormally thin bodies are the norm and being a size 12 is obese. Articles on dieting, exercise and cosmetic surgery encourage girls to attempt to achieve impossible goals.

Often the images that girls aspire to are not even real. Beauty today is a product of technology. In this digital age photo manipulation is more prevalent than ever. Props create illusions. Airbrushing takes away any lines or blemishes. A little digital pixie dust makes a model's eyes bluer, her teeth whiter, her leg slimmer. The power of computer technology improves light, color and contrast in photos not to mention thighs and heads.

Actress Jennifer Aniston was a victim of media manipulation when she appeared on the cover of *Redbook* magazine. She complained to *Us Weekly* that her whole body was put together like a jigsaw puzzle. The pants and her left hand with the wedding band were from one picture. Her right arm which was discolored and thickened was from another, her head from yet another, her shirt was painted on and her hair was changed. When Kate Winslet was overly slenderized on the cover of *GQ* she complained that the retouching was excessive. "I do not look like that," she was quoted as saying in the *The Daily Mail,* "and more importantly, I don't desire to look like that."[4]

The Media and Eating Disorders

Girls living in houses with a television are three times more likely to show symptoms of eating disorders than girls who do not. A study in the *British Journal of Psychiatry* showed that before television was introduced in Fiji in 1995 the number of girls who used self-induced vomiting to control their weight was zero. After three years of television the number was up to 11 per cent. By the end of the study, 69% of girls said they had gone on diets to lose weight and 74% said they thought they were too big or fat.[5]

Girls watch television, see movies and read magazines and compare themselves to the images they see. When girls don't see themselves in the media, they don't blame the media. They think that there is something wrong with them—and then try to change themselves. They want wider eyes, longer legs, smaller feet, firmer thighs, longer nails and bigger breasts. Most of all, they want to be thin. The media reinforces a culture that dismisses, disrespects and disempowers girls and women. By focusing on specific body parts, the media dissects women's bodies and encourages the dissociation from their bodies that most women feel. The images, texts and practices selected for use by the media encourage girls and women to be overly concerned with their appearance (and to require all their advertisers' products) and less concerned with their own values, qualities, characteristics, skills and talents. The media promotes what psychologist Dr. Margo Maine describes as *Body Wars* against girls' and women's bodies.[6] As long as girls are preoccupied with waging war against their bodies they cannot get on with their lives.

THE MEDIA'S MOST CHERISHED BODY MYTHS

➢ Beauty is a woman's principal project in life.

➢ Thinness is necessary for success and goodness.

➢ It is natural and acceptable for a woman to be self-conscious, anxious and ashamed of her body.

➢ Fat is a sign of personal responsibility for weakness, failure and helplessness.

➢ A winner can and should control, transform and renew herself through the technology of fashion, dieting, exercise and cosmetic surgery.

---

4 Kate Betts. "The Man Who Makes the Pictures Perfect," NY Times, February 2, 2003

5 Anne E. Becker, Rebecca A. Burwell, David B. Herzog, Paul Hamburg and Stephen E. Gilman. "Eating behaviours and attitudes following prolonged exposure to television among ethnic Fijian adolescent girls," *British Journal of Psychiatry*, 180: 509 – 514, Jun 2002

6 Margo Maine, PhD. *Body Wars: Making Peace with Women's Bodies.* Carlsbad, CA: Gurze Books, 2000

TV TURNOFF WEEK

Each April people around the world make a conscious decision to turn off their televisions sets and not play computer or video games or watch videos for a week. *TV Turnoff Week* provides an opportunity to evaluate the role that television programs, commercials and movies play in children's and adolescents' lives:

➢ How much time do children and adolescents watch TV?

➢ What shows are they watching?

➢ Who are they watching them with?

➢ Are there family rules about watching television?

➢ Does television take away from physical activity, family or social time or reading and hobbies?

➢ What are children and parents doing during TV Turnoff Week when they can't watch television?

➢ What changes would you like to make?

➢ How can you make them?

MEDIA LITERACY

National Film Board of Canada briefing notes (1993-1994)

All media productions present a point of view about the world that is manifested through the choices of the people who make them. These choices involve:

➢ What story will be told or reported?

➢ From whose perspective will it be presented?

➢ How will it be filmed? (camera placement, lighting, framing)

➢ What sort of music will be used, if any?

➢ Whose voice will we hear?

➢ What will the intended message be?

In order to understand the media's point of view we need to ask:

➢ Who has created the images?

➢ Who is doing the speaking?

➢ Whose viewpoint is not heard?

➢ From whose perspective does the camera frame the events?

➢ Who owns the medium?

➢ What is our role as spectators in identifying with or questioning what we see and hear?

Media Literacy

When we watch television, read magazines and newspapers, and surf the net we need to know how to 'read' the messages in these visual images just as we need to know how to read the words on a page. A media literate person doesn't know all the answers, but knows how to ask the right questions.

Media literacy is a way of teaching—using the media and their messages to help girls learn basic skills such as critical thinking, evaluating information, and detecting bias and persuasion. Then they can better understand and navigate our viewing culture in order to identify, analyze and challenge the beliefs around thinness that the media teaches and continually reinforces.

Media literacy is also about knowing how to create media messages in whatever format—infomercials, newsletters, videos, etc.—so that girls can understand how the media manipulates meaning, how they reorganize and reconstruct reality. When girls learn what goes into producing a media message, they also learn what's left out of the final product that the audience sees—and that helps them realize that all media messages they see are constructed. Somebody made them. They didn't just happen.

BECOMING MEDIA LITERATE

Have girls choose a television show they really like. Have them answer the questions listed below as they watch it. They may have to watch the show more than once. Discuss the answers in class, in a group or individually.

- ➢ What is the name of the show?
- ➢ What is the show about?
- ➢ Who are the main characters?
- ➢ What do the male characters tell us about how men are supposed to be?
- ➢ What do the female characters tell us about how women are supposed to be?
- ➢ What messages does the show give us about being male and being female?
- ➢ What messages about body image and what standard of beauty do the characters in this show reflect?
- ➢ Does the show include any characters of different races? How are they portrayed?
- ➢ Does the show include any characters who are fat or disabled?
- ➢ If so, how are they portrayed?
- ➢ If you were the director, how would you portray the women in the show?
- ➢ If you were the director, how would your show include a wide range of people?

BUILDING INDIVIDUAL POWERS OF DISCRIMINATION

➤ Using TV or video clips, and magazines, and/or newspaper pictures:

- Make a chart of the similarities and differences in appearance and body size of the 'good' characters and the 'bad' characters.
- Make note of the type of camera shots used for the 'good' and 'bad' characters.
- Compare these characters with yourselves, your peers and your family members.

➤ Select pictures from newspapers and magazines that show the difference between posed and natural photographs of boys and girls and men and women. Describe what is emphasized in each.

➤ Have girls physically imitate the ways in which men and women are positioned in fashion advertisements and features.

- How does this make them feel?
- Do the poses help or hinder the messages?
- Who is being targeted?
- Are there consistent differences between male and female poses? If so, why? What messages are women and men likely or supposed to get from these differences?

➤ Cut and paste pictures of families from magazines and newspapers. Collect photographs of real families. Compare the family structures and the activities of each member. Discuss how and why the media portray families differently from real life families.

➤ View several clips from popular cartoons. Classify the cartoons as violent and nonviolent. Focus on the behavior of the characters.

- Why and how is violence used?
- Are the characters male or female?
- Who is the victim?
- How would the character act if the sex were reversed?
- Can the same situation be solved in a non-violent way?

➤ Select several commercials. Identify whether certain commercials appeal to boys or girls and why. What does the advertisement tell you about each sex? Is this true? Is the voice of authority in the background male or female? Why? Make a list of things boys and girls like to do. Compare this list with what is shown in commercials. Do commercial children participate in the same activities as real children? Are boys and girls shown playing together? Do the same thing with magazines.

➤ Ask students to bring in images of women, youth, teens, elderly, minorities, men and people with disabilities. Each week choose one of these groups. Have students bring in examples from magazines, film, TV, bumper stickers, newspapers, fiction, billboards and the internet. What are the prevailing media messages surrounding and reinforcing stereotypes? What, if any, are the alternatives to these prevailing images?

Web Literacy

The Internet is often the first choice today for girls when they are trying to find information about issues that are of concern to them. There are millions of sites on the Web containing various combinations of text, images, links, music and/or downloadable softwear. While traditional sources of information such as newspapers, book publishers or material developed by institutions are checked to make sure the material is accurate, anyone can post information on the Internet. Many girls, including those who are secondary students, believe that information presented on the Internet is true. We need to teach web literacy in the same way we teach media literacy so girls can evaluate the information on the Internet to determine if it is credible.

Cyberspace's 5 W's plus...

- ➢ Who is the source?
- ➢ What am I getting?
- ➢ When was it created?
- ➢ Where am I?
- ➢ Why am I there?

  and...

- ➢ How can I distinguish quality information from junk?

Pro-anorexia Web sites

While many Web sites contain information that is not accurate some, such as pro-anorexia Web sites, are downright harmful. Pro-anorexia Web sites reinforce and encourage anorexia and bulimia. They use message boards and online discussion forums which explain how girls can hide their condition from friends and family, the best way to use laxatives and how girls can make themselves vomit. Some of these Web sites contain 'online journals,' dieting tips, and various types of deadly competitions. News groups and mailing lists may be offered to encourage girls not to eat or not to give up their anorexic behavior.

The information presented on these websites tends to normalize anorexia and bulimia and make them less shocking. Girls and women give each other information on how to become anorexic or make their conditions worse. They promote competition and glamorize the disorders. They also keep girls and women in denial so they won't address their medical, psychological and emotional problems by getting help.

MEDIA ACTIVISM

Media activism refers to efforts to change the messages that are portrayed by the media. You can encourage girls to become media activists in the following ways:

> Encourage girls to speak out. Students in a British Columbia middle-school asked Coca-Cola to remove what they saw as subliminal images of curvaceous women from onsite pop dispensers, saying it was wrong to use sexual messages to sell products in school. The students were offended by the images and felt the advertising on the school's machines was unethical, insulting and degrading.

> The media's main goal is to deliver audiences to advertisers. When we as consumers express our disapproval of a program or advertisement, media producers take notice because their profits depend on us. Encourage girls to write letters to newspapers, television and radio stations, and transit companies to protest or praise media products that have been identified and analyzed as conveying or contradicting undesirable unhealthy messages about women and girls. In 1998, Hershey Foods Corporation decided to advertise a chocolate bar with the slogan "You can never be too rich or too thin." ANAD (Anorexia Nervosa and Related Disorders) protested with a petition and letter-writing campaign. The advertisement was withdrawn. Our comments do make a difference.

> Encourage girls to write letters praising media outlets and companies for their efforts in empowering girls and women and promoting a healthy sense of their bodies. One such company, for example, is the Body Shop which promoted Ruby—a full-figured Rubenesque Barbie-like doll reclining on a love seat and encouraging women to "love your body." Ruby emphasizes that there are 3 billion women who don't look like supermodels and only 8 who do.

> Encourage girls to write letters about how they feel about the pressure to be thin. By speaking out, girls validate themselves and provide a voice for other girls who feel the way that they do. When Elise Mallory whose letter is featured on page 110 wrote to the Vancouver Sun she was astonished to find that so many girls could relate to what she was saying.

> Organize a petition. In 1991, Virginie Lariviere, a 13 year old girl from Quebec started a national petition to end television violence because she was convinced that it had been a factor in the rape and murder of her younger sister. In 1992 she presented 1.2 million signatures to then-Prime Minister Brian Mulroney. Her petition pushed TV violence to the top of the public agenda and was the catalyst for the rewriting of the Canadian Association of Broadcasters' Violence Code.

WRITING AN EFFECTIVE COMMENT LETTER

Reprinted with adaptations by permission of MediaWatch Canada

- ➤ Write as soon as possible. The information will be fresh in your mind and you will be taking advantage of the energy from your initial reaction. Encourage friends to also write.

- ➤ Direct your letter to the appropriate contact.

- ➤ Identify yourself. Include your name, address, city, province or state, postal or zip code and phone number. Anonymous letters are not taken seriously.

- ➤ Identify the medium and format. If you are writing about a TV commercial, for example, indicate when you saw it and on which station. For a magazine article indicate which issue. Try to include a copy of the newspaper article that you are writing about.

- ➤ Write persuasively. You want to sway the reader to be open to your point of view so that he or she will take action.

- ➤ Criticize constructively. Focus criticism on the issue, not the organization or individual. Be specific about what you find offensive and why.

- ➤ Give praise where it is due. If you can find something positive to say about the service or product or presentation that you are objecting to, add these details. (Remember roses and onions.)

- ➤ Be clear. Explain your position in a clear and concise manner. Try not to assume that the reader observes the same negative aspects that you do.

- ➤ Suggest alternatives. If you can think of an alternative image or reference that you find acceptable, describe it. Some media producers are unaware of the issues that concern us and appreciate positive and specific suggestions.

- ➤ Remind the recipient of what's at stake. You, your friends and family are part of the market that the advertiser or broadcaster wants to reach. If you are considering a boycott of the product involved, mention that in your letter.

- ➤ Ask for a response. Follow up with another letter or phone call if necessary.

- ➤ Copy and circulate. In addition to copying to MediaWatch, ask yourself who else might be interested.

- ➤ Pat yourself on the back. Most people complain but don't do anything about it. You have taken a proactive step in curtailing the negative images of women and girls in the media. In doing so you have nurtured *girlpower*.

SAMPLE COMMENT LETTER

Reprinted with permission of MediaWatch Canada

Always include your name, address, phone number and the date.
Anonymous letters are not taken seriously.

Sarah Serious Complainant
1267 Angry Drive
Somewhere BC V2A 1L9
March 8, 2000

Ms Laura Dallal
Advertising Standards Canada (ASC)
350 Bloor Street East, Suite 402
Toronto, ON   M4W 1H5

Dear Ms Dallal:

I am writing to express my concern over an advertisement for Fetish perfume that appeared on the outside of a Translink bus in Vancouver. In the ad a white, blond, very young and very thin woman is featured sporting the typical blank, passive look, pouting mouth and make-up bruised eyes. Here neck and face are strewn with sparkles (presumably where the perfume would be applied). The ad copy reads: "Fetish #16: Apply generously to your neck so that he can smell the scent as you shake your head 'no'."

I find the imagery in this ad very disturbing. *NO means NO* campaigns have been working hard to create an understanding of sexual consent and to make us aware of the reality of date rape. The imagery in the Fetish ad implies that women are constantly sexual, that they like being able to "turn a man on," and that NO is a part of the ritual of flirtation. This feeds the idea that rape victims are actually "asking for it" and minimizes and trivializes the very real problem of violence against women.

I hope that you will assist us in getting this ad pulled as soon as possible as it is in a very public place. I look forward to hearing from you.

Sincerely

Sarah Serious Complainant

cc. Houbigant (Fetish), Toronto Transit Commission, Translink, MediaWatch

When notified of the consumer complaint, the advertiser voluntarily withdrew the advertisement even before the ASC Council heard the formal complaint and ruled that the *Fetish* ad violated their Advertising Code of Ethics.

THE DEFINITION OF *PRETTY* SHOULD COVER ALL SHAPES

Make sure that you put your full name, address and daytime telephone number in the letter when you are writing to the editor of a newspaper. Often they will phone you to verify that this opinion is indeed yours.

Elise Mallory
2639 152nd Avenue
Langley, BC   V2K lR7
(604) 555-1214
January 22, 2000

The Editor
The Vancouver Sun
1-200 Granville Street
Vancouver, BC V6C 3N3

Dear Sir or Madam:

This is for all the girls who are overweight or plain looking: We are all in this war together.

What has the world done for normal girls? Except to give us pictures of people we will never be and crush our dreams under piles of magazines, nothing. Television and movies show us "perfection." Why can't everybody be perfect? But we are either too heavy or too plain; too quiet or too loud. These are just some of the rules dished out in piles of beauty magazines and romance movies.

Many people don't know what it is like to be ugly or to consider yourself ugly. But what is pretty? Is it the bones you see on such shows as Friends and Ally McBeal? I like these shows and have nothing against their humor, but what are they telling us—you can't act unless you are skinny? This is the message I get.

Girls become anorexic so that they can be models and be liked. We cringe at how skinny these moneymaking girls are, but underneath we long to be like that, too. People cry themselves to sleep at night after being teased about their weight.

If a show came out with actors and actresses in a variety of shapes and sizes, it could change the definition of pretty.

We are the ones staying home on Friday nights, not getting invited to parties—all because of the perfect people. I would be skinny right now if it were not for my lack of self-discipline. To be skinny is to be pretty, to be loved.

So the next time you watch a TV show filled with skinny people who get everything they want or read a magazine on beauty and makeup, stop and think how many people's dreams are being crushed under the weight of the world.

Don't look at what is on the outside, but to what is on the inside. They haven't made rules as to what is needed to be pretty inside.

Elise Mallory, Age 14

This actual letter is reprinted here with the kind permission of Elise Mallory and her parents.

109.

MEDIA ADVOCACY

From Media Advocacy Manual – American Public Health Association

Media advocacy refers to efforts to use the media to promote an issue in order to educate the public, sway public opinion towards or against a certain point of view and influence policy-makers and encourage social change.

Encourage girls to become media advocates by writing letters to the editors of magazines, television news programs and newspapers, sending out press releases, giving interviews and writing 'Op Ed' or opinion articles for the editorial pages of newspapers.

➢ Establish what your goal is: bringing attention to a specific issue; wanting the community to take action on an issue or trying to change a policy.

➢ Design the message: Make it clear and simple as well as powerful, persuasive and compelling to catch the eye of the audience.

➢ Personalize the message by putting a human face on it.

➢ Make sure that the message targets the intended audience.

➢ Ask yourself:

- What is the problem you are highlighting?

- Is there a solution to it? If so, what is it?

- Who can make the solution possible? Whose support do you need?

- What do you need to do or say to get the attention of those who can make the solution happen?

GO GIRLS™ — An Exciting Example

GO GIRLS™ (Giving Our Girls Inspiration and Resources for Lasting Self-Esteem!) integrates media awareness and analysis, media activism and advocacy as well as relational group work. The 12-week curriculum focuses on key issues such as body image, media awareness and the power of speaking out. When the *GO GIRLS*™ program in Vancouver, Washington ended in 1998 the group stayed together. Over the next five-year the girls took aim at media and social messages that emphasize unrealistic ideals. They spoke to students about becoming critical thinkers and aware consumers and observers. The video they made in their efforts to persuade retailer Nordstrom to include size and shape diversity in their junior clothing displays became a major media activism campaign that brought about an awareness of size diversity. What started as a goal to have junior clothes for girls of all sizes at different stores became an important social change. The girls celebrated their high school graduation in 2003 by sponsoring an educational fashion show that featured size-diversity. Hats off to Deanna Green the project coordinator!!

STRESS

Risk Factors Addressed:
Body Dissatisfaction
Social Comparison
High exposure to unhealthy and
   unrealistically thin body image ideals
Low Self-Esteem

It's impossible for girls to grow up without ever experiencing stress. They see their parents run short of money, lose their jobs, try to juggle childcare and work outside the home, and bring home the effects of stress from the workplace. When jobs or life situations cause families to relocate, or when there is divorce or a death in the family, everyone feels the stress of change. Violence and war on television and the constant threat of terrorism create additional stressors.

Adolescent girls have their own stressors to contend with. They have to deal with the physical changes in their bodies, insecurities about their appearance, and the societal pressure to conform to an ideal shape. Girls have to negotiate the rituals and routines of school life including studying for exams, completing projects and the pressure to achieve. The ups and downs of friendships, emerging sexuality, and relationships with boys are also stressors. So, too, are the need to be perfect and the amount of energy that goes into worrying about what other people think of you. Being bullied, teased and harassed can be major stressors. Girls have to deal with family conflicts over taking care of siblings, wanting independence from parents who are afraid to let go, illness, losses of friendships and pets and (sometimes) of family members, accidents and other physical or emotional situations that have long term effects.

Stress can result from a build-up of everyday worries. It can also result from having to do something different—such as moving on from elementary to middle school to junior high and then on to high school, beginning a new job or relationship, moving to a new home or starting a new school or work assignment.

Not all stress is about bad things—even good things can be stressful. No matter how excited we are by something new or by some of the changes in our lives, we often feel insecure at the beginning as we adjust to these new situations and learn new skills. Our level of stress increases when we are not allowed to acknowledge these feelings or if we place a lot of expectations on ourselves. Stress becomes a problem when we can't turn off our reaction and our bodies remain at a high level of arousal for long periods of time. When this happens our muscles become overloaded, our emotions become strained or go out of control, our immune system becomes less effective and we become exhausted.

When girls have reached the limits of their abilities to cope, they react to stress by sleeping less, smoking, skipping school, withdrawing from their families and friends and being critical and judgmental of themselves and of others. Some girls use alcohol and/or drugs as a way of getting rid of unpleasant feelings. Many others use food and behaviors around food and weight as a way of coping with stress and with responses to stress such as anxiety, depression, mood swings and panic attacks. Some girls binge in order to stuff down or anesthetize their feelings, some anesthetize their feelings by bingeing and then by discharging them through purging, and some tighten their restrictions when they feel out of control. The preoccupation with weight and with pursuing thinness initially gives girls a false sense of control and takes the focus off what is really going on.

Bodily/Physical and Emotional Responses to Stress

Acne	Increased heart rate
Increased blood pressure	Indigestion
Tired or low energy levels	Difficulty breathing
Cold or warm hands	Sweating
Weak knees, clenched jaws	Flushed face
Tight back, shoulders and neck	Nausea, dizziness, headaches
Loss of or increased appetite	Difficulty sleeping
Lack of interest in everyday activities	Restlessness
Decreased self-esteem	Difficulty making decisions
Loss of memory	Decreased concentration
Disorganized	Withdrawal from friends
Anxiety, depression, panic attacks	Moodiness, tears, irritability
Nightmares	Increase in nervous habits
Compulsive overeating, dieting	Bingeing and purging

STRESS MANAGEMENT

We need to provide girls with healthy ways of dealing with the stressors in their lives before they are deflected onto their bodies and manifested through body dissatisfaction, eating disorder behaviors, depression and anxiety.

Healthy Eating

Good nutrition can help girls balance their moods. For example sugar and caffeine increase stress because they are stimulants. Eating small amounts at regular intervals keeps your blood sugar from dropping and therefore is helpful in managing anxiety as are foods rich in calcium.

Physical Activity

Physical activity helps girls feel calmer, energized and more relaxed. This is because natural chemicals like endorphins are released into the body and help relax the brain and provide a sense of well-being.

A Good Night's Sleep

Researchers found that students who reported getting a good night's sleep coped better on final exams and interviewing for graduate programs than those whose sleep was disturbed. The students who slept well tended to focus on tasks rather than on their emotions during stressful situations. This helped them sleep better and in turn helped them cope. Sleep even served as a kind of escape from a stressful day.

Quiet Time

Having quiet time helps girls counteract the stimulation around them and allows them to refocus on themselves. Quiet time can include reading a book, writing in a journal or practicing relaxation skills.

Relaxation Skills

Imagine that your sense of self is a ball of wool. Every time you focus outward on what people want, what people think and fulfilling your 'shoulds' you unravel the ball of wool. The degree to which it is unraveled at the end of the day represents your disconnection from your body and your self. Relaxation skills allow girls to rewind the ball of wool and to reconnect with their bodies by bringing the focus back to themselves.

> ➢ Meditation helps girls quiet their thoughts by focusing completely on just one thing and therefore excluding all outside thoughts and stimulation for a long period of time such as 20 to 30 minutes.

> Progressive Muscle Relaxation (PMR) is a purely physical technique for helping girls relax their bodies when their muscles are tense.

> Deep Breathing works well in conjunction with other relaxation techniques such as PMR, relaxation imagery and meditation to reduce stress.

Problem Solving and Decision Making Skills

Good problem solving and decision making skills help girls reduce stress by helping them take charge of their lives and feel more in control.

> Planning is a way of managing stress by preparing for it.

> Prioritizing helps find out what is important and helps put things into perspective.

Developing Supportive Relationships

Supportive relationships are powerful stress busters. Women and girls respond to stress differently than men do. Until recently it was believed when people experienced stress, they triggered a hormonal cascade that stimulated the body to either stand and fight or flee as fast as possible. However, a study published in 2000 by the American Psychological Association found when the hormone oxytocin is released as part of the stress response in a woman, it buffers the fight or flight response and encourages her to tend children and gather with other women instead. When she engages in this 'tending and befriending' more oxytocin is released which further counters stress and produces a calming effect. Estrogen enhances this process. Getting together with friends does not work with men because the high levels of testosterone they produce when they are under stress counter the effects of oxytocin.[1]

Social ties reduce our risk of disease by lowering our blood pressure, heart rate and cholesterol. The ongoing Nurses' Study established in 1976 by Dr. Frank Speizer at Harvard Medical School found the more friends women had, the less likely they were to develop physical impairments as they aged and the more likely they were to lead a joyful life.

Recognizing and Dealing with the *grungies and* Communication Skills

Recognizing and dealing with the grungies and building good communication skills are important to maintaining healthy relationships and therefore in reducing stress. Girls who have healthy relationships can support each other. Girls who experience conflicts in their relationships experience an increase in stress.

---

1 S.E. Taylor, L.C. Klein, B.P. Lewis, T.L. Gruenwald, R.A.R. Gurung & J.A. Updegraff. "Biobehavioral Responses to Stress in Females: Tend-and-Befriend, Not Fight or Flight," American Psychological Association, *Psychological Review*, Vol. 107, No. 3, 411-429, 2000

PRACTICING STRESS MANAGEMENT TECHNIQUES

Centering—Breathing Out the Stress

Have the girls sit comfortably in a chair with their feet on the floor, or lie on the floor.

➤ Ask the girls to put their hand on their bellies, just below the navel.

➤ Ask the girls to close their eyes and begin to breathe. Have them feel their bellies move up as they breathe in and down as they breathe out. Tell them if this is uncomfortable, they should breathe as far down as they are comfortable doing. [Some girls may have difficulty breathing into their bellies. This is often the case for girls who are anorexic or bulimic and find it scary to experience the fullness of their bellies which they perceive as fat.]

➤ Say to the girls:

- Each time you breathe, imagine the sound of the ocean coming in and going out, or a ribbon of color moving up and down.

- If you have a thought, let it float away.

- Imagine each time you breathe out, that you are sending the stress out of your body through your fingers and toes.

➤ Continue the exercise for a few minutes having the girls breathe out their stress.

➤ Ask the girls to imagine a place where they feel relaxed or a beautiful clear blue sky with several puffy, white clouds floating along with the air currents. Have them hop aboard a cloud and let themselves float along totally supported by the soft enveloping cloud. They have nothing to do now but relax, float and enjoy the ride.

➤ Tell the girls when they slowly open their eyes they will remember what it is like to be in that place.

➤ Encourage the girls to practice this exercise several times a day so when they need it they already know how to use it.

Progressive Muscle Relaxation (PMR)

Have the girls sit in the chair comfortably with their feet on the floor and their eyes closed. (You could also have them lie on the floor.) Take them through the following muscle tightening sequence. With each one ask them to hold for a count of ten and relax. Keep reminding them to breathe. Tell them to…

➤ Tighten the muscles in their toes.

➤ Point their toes to their nose and tighten the muscles in their calves.

➤ Press their legs together and tighten their leg muscles.

➤ Tighten the muscles in their buttocks.

> Tighten the muscles in their stomachs.

> Tighten their right fist.

> Tighten their left fist.

> Press their arms against their bodies and tighten their arm muscles.

> Scrunch their shoulders up to their ears.

> Scrunch up their faces.

> Now tense up all the muscles in the body.

> Now take a deep breath and hold it. Note all the minimum tensions. Exhale and feel the relaxation and calmness developing. Let the relaxation spread through the arms and the rest of the body.

Drawing a Stress Tree—Identifying and Prioritizing Stressors

Materials: drawing paper or flip chart paper / felt pens

This exercise helps distinguish between long and short-term stresses and those things that are in and out of their control. It lets girls know that many of their stressors are common to other girls. It gives them an opportunity to brainstorm on healthy coping strategies.

> Give each girl a sheet of drawing paper.

> Have the girls draw a large tree trunk.

> Have the girls think of things, people or situations that cause them to feel stressed.

> Ask them to draw and label a leaf for every one of these situations.

> When girls are finished with the tree, have them make one list of short-term stressors and one of long-term stressors.

> Have the girls number the stressors according to how important they are to them. This will help them develop a sense of priorities.

> Divide the girls into small groups or groups of three. Have them compare their lists. Ask them to make a list of the stresses that they have in common, and a list of the ones that are different.

> Have them share their answers with the larger group.

> Discuss healthy ways in which girls can deal with stress. Remember that they have to take small steps and that nobody can fail

BULLYING

Risk Factors Addressed:
Loss of Voice
Changes in Relationships
Body Dissatisfaction
Self-Esteem

A group of grade seven girls sat in front of me at a community talk in a small town. They hung on to my every word. The moment we took a break they rushed up to me. They wanted to talk about the two girls in their class who were calling them names and picking on them. They couldn't talk to their teacher even though they really liked him because one of the bullies was his daughter. When I asked if they could talk to the school nurse, they laughed and said that the school nurse was married to their teacher so the bully was her daughter, too. We talked about the lack of safety these girls felt. We brainstormed about how they could enlist their mothers and how all of them could approach the school. Then we worked on how they could support each other and considered some strategies that they could each try.

Bullying is one of the most frequent and difficult situations that girls (and boys) have to deal with in school today. An incident of bullying takes place once every seven minutes. While it usually only lasts about thirty-seven seconds, its emotional effects have a much longer impact on the victims and on others who witness the bullying. Bullying affects the physical, social and psychological safety of girls and boys at school. It can create a climate of fear that becomes an obstacle to learning and to healthy development. Its physical and emotional effects can be deadly as evidenced by more and more incidents are reported of girls and boys committing suicide because they were bullied and teased.

Bullying does not happen because of miscommunication between two people. Very rarely is it a one-time-only event and never is it accidental. Bullies seek power. They intend to put the victim in distress and do emotional or physical harm. It's not only their frequent and repeated attacks that are harmful, but also the anticipatory terror that can have long-term effects.

Boys bully other boys and they bully girls in order to elevate their own status and increase their sense of adequacy. Girls bully girls who they see as a threat to their relationships with other girls and to their relationships with boyfriends. While both girls and boys engage in each of the different kinds of bullying behaviors, they tend to focus on those that are congruent with their gender culture and development.

Physical Bullying is usually done by boys—although this is growing among girls. They kick and hit the victim and/or take and damage the victim's property. These bullies become more aggressive as they get older.

Verbal Bullying usually takes the form of teasing and name-calling in order to hurt and humiliate the victim. Bullies emphasize whatever makes the victim different from his or her peers. They focus on areas where they know their victim is vulnerable. When girls tease each other their aggression targets body size and personal characteristics. The worst thing they can call one another is 'fat.' For many girls being teased about being fat is a trigger to dieting and is therefore a big risk factor in developing an eating disorder. When boys tease each other their verbal aggression often takes the form of homophobic and misogynist comments such as 'fag,' 'wuss' and 'girl.'

Relational Bullying is the dark side of friendship. It is most often done by girls who exclude other girls from their peer groups, spread nasty rumors about them, tell secrets about them, tease them and frame them and set them up for punishment. It is indirect and is devastating to girls who are rejected from their peer groups at the time that they need them the most.

Sexual Harassment is also a form of bullying. In elementary school girls are called 'sluts,' 'whores' (or 'hos'), 'cunts' and 'bitches' by boys who pinch their breasts and lift their skirts. In many high schools girls can't walk down the halls without being grabbed and groped. Girls who beat up other girls (whom they label as sluts and who they see as threats to their boyfriends) are also practicing a form of sexual harassment.

A COMPREHENSIVE AND COLLABORATIVE PLAN...

➢ Creates a shared understanding about the nature of bullying and its effects on the lives of individual students and the school community.

➢ Assists members of the school community in acquiring the specific knowledge, skills and language to respond to bullying.

➢ Is proactive and not punitive.

➢ Provides a framework for bringing the plan to life.

➢ Directs the development of a wide array of prevention and intervention strategies.

Students who are being bullied often become reluctant to come to school, or to walk there and back all alone. They have headaches, stomachaches and other bodily symptoms. They show signs of depression such as low energy, difficulty in sleeping, and eating too much or too little. They don't want to talk about what's happening in school and if they do, they don't want parental or teacher intervention because they are afraid of being singled out and being made subject to worse treatment.

Students can't stop bullying on their own. When we talk of zero tolerance but don't enforce it, we teach students that no one will stand up for them. As a result, they often don't report these incidents. They feel embarrassed and humiliated, are afraid to be seen as 'squealers', and fear retribution that is ten times worse than the original bullying.

Parents can't stop bullying on their own. When individual parents complain to teachers and schools that their child is being bullied they are sometimes seen as the problem instead of the bully and their child suffers the consequences of their complaint.

Implementing a Comprehensive, Collaborative School-Wide Plan

In order to put an end to bullying, there must be a comprehensive and collaborative school-wide plan in place that involves parents, teachers, students, support staff, administration and the community. The parents must support the administration even if it is hard for them to acknowledge their child may be a bully and the administration must support the teachers even when parents complain that the bully can't possibly be their child. All of the adults involved with the school must provide students with safety if they inform on the perpetrators. This means guaranteeing students the bullying will stop; that it will be stopped in such a way that no one knows who reported it, and that the bully will be treated firmly but with understanding. If the adults don't follow up with action, then the students will feel not only unsafe but also betrayed not matter how good the intentions of the plan.

Developing and implementing a comprehensive and collaborative plan takes time and commitment. While there is often a tendency to 'fix' things by immediately putting a plan into place, without the commitment of everyone involved it falls apart the first time it is not supported. For a comprehensive plan to work everyone must buy into it. Thus the planning process is just as important as the plan itself. The planning process brings together different groups of people, teaches them a different way of interacting and builds trust by ensuring that everyone is committed, and that everyone's voice is heard and respected. Once the mechanisms are in place for a collaborative and comprehensive plan for addressing bullying, the process can easily be applied to addressing eating disorders prevention and other health and social risks that girls and boys are vulnerable to by creating a safe environment.

Steps for Developing a Comprehensive and Collaborative Plan

Establish a working group that includes parents, teachers, administrators, support staff, students, school nurses, school liaison officers and other community members.

➤ Involve parents.

➤ Involve students.

➤ Create a *School Statement For Bullying Prevention*.

➤ Build a *Supervision Plan*.

➤ Build a *Complaint Plan*.

➤ Build the *Response Plan*.

➤ Implement and monitor the *School Plan*.

➤ Address bullying prevention through classroom lessons.

➤ Support students and staff.

Helping Girls Deal with Bullying

Although we as individuals acting alone cannot stop bullying behavior, we can help girls avoid situations where they will be bullied, support girls who are at risk, teach them skills and techniques for dealing with bullying situations and help girls deal with the effects when they have been bullied.

➤ Help girls develop social and interpersonal skills and provide them with opportunities for practice. One good way to do this is through participation in groups (see the JUST FOR GIRLS program in RESOURCES).

➤ Talk about bullying.

➤ Practice fighting back.

When Someone is Being Bullied:

➤ Encourage the girl to talk about the bullying. Let her know bullying is hurtful and that she has the right to be safe when she comes to school.

➤ Encourage details: What do people call you? What do they do? Talking about bullying in a safe atmosphere helps validate the individual, lets her know that she is not alone, helps her get rid of the shame and lets her know it is not her fault.

➤ Describe bullying as an issue of power. Girls need to know it has nothing to do with their adequacy or inadequacy as a friend or how they look.

➤ Describe bullying as a school and community problem. Talk about who needs to be involved in order to stop it.

➤ Explore who can help, who is safe and who is not.

➤ Encourage girls to travel in pairs. They are less likely to be bullied if they are with a friend. Providing and facilitating girls' groups in your school or community is a good way to help girls make friends, build alliances and support one another.

Fighting Back: Role-Playing Situations and Solutions

Bullies usually stop if we don't react to the content of what they are saying. Our reaction is what fuels their aggression. Review the section on Communication on pages 62–68. Practice by having a girl be the bully and you be the victim, then reverse roles.

➤ Each time the 'bully' says something, you (the victim) repeat: "Stop, I don't like what you are saying." or "Stop, I don't like how you're acting." (It's tempting to respond to the content, so be careful you say the same thing over and over again until she stops.) See "Yes but…" on page

➤ Ask her what it felt like to be the bully and what it felt like when you kept repeating "Stop, I don't like what you are saying" or "Stop, I don't like how you're acting."

➤ Change roles. Encourage her to stand up straight and look directly at you. Have her practice saying "Stop, I don't like what you are saying" or "Stop, I don't like how you're acting."

➤ Have girls role play how they can support each other. Repeat the exercise above but this time have the support person say, "Stop, I don't like what you are saying to her" or "Stop, I don't like how you are acting towards her."

Sources:

Focus on Bullying: A Prevention Program for Elementary School Communities. British Columbia Ministry of Education & Ministry of the Attorney General.

Gesele Lajoie, Alyson McLellan & Cindi Seddon, *Take Action Against Bullying.* Bully B'Ware Productions, Coquitlam, BC, 1997

APPLYING PREVENTION SKILLS

& STRATEGIES

There are many different ways we can apply the skills and strategies presented in this manual. We can take advantage of teachable moments, integrate our skills into existing programs or classroom lessons, prepare specific lessons, offer presentations, facilitate groups and work with schools and communities to create body-friendly environments. We can practice our skills with just about anything that we do. As long as we remember the *Golden Rules of Prevention*, we can't go wrong.

THE GOLDEN RULES OF PREVENTION

ADDRESS the changes in girls' bodies (Body Issues)

ADDRESS the changes in girls' lives (Self Issues)

INCORPORATE the basic elements of prevention:
> Teach girls about the *grungies*
> Fight the power of appearance
> Promote size acceptance

HONOR female development and culture

No Place for Eating Disorders Information

In every prevention workshop I facilitate the question that always arises is where information about eating disorders fits in. The answer is simple: it doesn't. Prevention takes place before the fact so knowing about the end result isn't necessary. Talking about anorexia or bulimia can be harmful because it can give girls—especially young girls—negative information about how to control their weight by starvation, purging and excessive exercise. Bringing in newspaper articles about young women who have eating disorders, having discussions about their experiences led by recovered peers or older girls, enacting plays about girls with eating disorders—all these may be harmful because they inadvertently glamorize and normalize eating disorder behaviors. These activities do not deter girls because they don't address the underlying issues that make girls vulnerable to developing eating disorders.

The closest I get, depending on the circumstances, is acknowledging that eating disorders do exist (we all know someone who has or had an eating disorder) and eating disorders occur when girls feel fat all the time and when their behaviors around food are out of control. In secondary schools I like to leave room for girls who might have an eating disorder or who are experimenting with the behaviors to come forward. When I do community presentations I always make sure there is no literature being handed out that describes eating disorder behaviors.

While the words 'eating disorders' rarely cross my lips, neither does the word 'obesity.' Talking about the dangers of being fat makes fat girls feel guilty and self-conscious about their size. Encouraging them to diet causes emotional and psychological harm, endangers their health and increases their risk of developing an eating disorder. It also reinforces societal prejudice towards people who are fat.

Teachable Moments

Once we have taught girls about the grungies we need to capitalize on the teachable moments that arise out of their everyday lives. When we hear someone tell herself she is fat, ugly, stupid or whatever other description leaves her feeling badly about herself, it's a good idea to stop whatever we are doing and to remind her about the grungies. This doesn't mean that we need to have a formal lesson. A short intervention will do. Saying "Hey, Kelly, sounds like you've just been hit by a grungie. What's underneath?" breaks the obsessive pattern and helps Kelly remember something else is going on. It gives her permission to talk about what is real at a time when there is a lot of social pressure on her to hold back. The more practice girls have decoding their grungies, the more aware of them they are going to become. The more opportunities girls have to express themselves or put feelings and opinions out, the less likely they are to redirect them against themselves and encode them in a language of fat.

Teachable moments happen all the time. When girls make comments about their bodies we can also talk about different body types and explore with them what body type they are and what they are trying to be. When girls are afraid to eat or are commenting on what other girls eat we can help them explore their fears. When they tease each other and/or when conflict arises we can help them express themselves directly. Above all, we can encourage girls to talk about their concerns. Dealing with something immediately and in the context of a real life situation is much more effective than any pre-planned lesson can be.

Planning Classroom Lessons

Whenever we lecture or talk at girls, they tune us out. Like us, girls learn best when their learning occurs in the context of their lives and experiences. We also need to give girls time to discuss the information that we present. This may mean we need to plan a follow-up session for questions they might want to raise after they have had time to think things over. If the material is sensitive in nature, it's a good idea to provide girls with a means of asking their questions anonymously—for example, writing them down and putting them into an envelope or basket where the questions can be drawn at random. Even if the girls seem to be open don't assume they will publicly share their deepest concerns.

Personalize information: Girls need information about metabolism and genetics, and about the changes in their bodies. They need to know what food really does so that they can debunk the myths of 'good food' and 'bad food'. During adolescence girls need to know about the changes in their lives, about sexuality and relationships and about the dangers of dieting. When we give girls information it is important that we personalize it. This doesn't mean we discuss the details of our eating disorder or dieting history or the current emotional situations in our lives. It means we selectively share ourselves in order to create safety and to encourage girls to share themselves.

Remember K.I.S.S.—Teach skills and present alternatives: Every time we provide girls with information about risk factors, we need to teach the complementary skills that will help them develop the resiliency to cope with these risks. For example, when we encourage girls to accept their bodies, we also need to teach them about body types and help them normalize fat so that it is not a character judgment but a description of size or component of food. When we talk about the influence of the media we need to teach girls media literacy skills and help them fight back against the power of appearance.

Balance lessons about body issues with lessons about self issues: We have a tendency to address eating disorder prevention solely in terms of body image and healthy eating. Remember the golden rules of prevention. Don't forget to plan lessons that address the changes in girls' lives. It might be helpful to alternate lessons about body issues and life issues in order to make sure that girls have a context for the changes that are happening to them and a language with which to describe them.

Teach girls about the *grungies*: If I had my way this would be a national campaign! Teaching girls about the grungies is the most effective way of helping them maintain their sense of self because it encourages them to address what's real instead of encoding the realities of their lives in the language of fat (or ugly or stupid) and then reacting to the fat instead of responding to the situation that caused the grungie.

Remember the context: It doesn't make sense for girls to learn about self esteem and then be teased by boys or by each other, or for them to learn about healthy eating when they are skipping lunch and/or intimidating or being intimidated by other girls about what they eat. When what we teach is in direct opposition to what is important to girls or to what they are doing, they either tune us out or feel guilty when they cannot comply. It doesn't change their behavior.

Include an activity: The best way girls learn is by doing, so they have a context that makes sense to them. Activities also reinforce the skills and concepts that you have taught. Remember to reassure girls that they cannot fail. Encourage curiosity. After the activity encourage the girls to talk about what it was like for them, where they were stuck and what they learned.

Encourage small group activities: This allows girls to help and to validate each other. Remember female culture. Girls are relational. Although we may get angry with them for what we perceive as chitchatting, a lot of valuable learning comes from the schmoozing they do. Small groups allow girls to help one another as well as validate each other. When you have finished the activity, encourage girls to talk about it.

Use handouts with sensitivity: Handouts are valuable resources because they give girls time to think about themselves and their issues. However, we never know what girls take in and what they do with the information or the feelings the information generates. It's helpful to discuss the handouts once girls have read them. This helps us find out where girls are stuck and what misconceptions exist. Sometimes when girls can't complete the handout, they give themselves a grungie and think they are stupid. Take care when you use handouts they do not become homework. We need to help girls associate learning about themselves with curiosity and not with failure and fear. This makes it safe for them no matter what they say or write.

Integrate the material into other lessons or situations: Teach about metabolism, genetics and set-point in science class. Look at different body types when you teach geography or social studies. Making history girl-friendly validates female culture and gives girls role models and heroes who are not thin movie stars or singers. Instead of focusing on battles and dates, look at whose voices are missing, and at what girls and women were doing in different time periods. Who are the Mothers of Confederation and who were the Canadian Famous Five? (No, they weren't rock groups!) What was life like for Martha Washington? Make sure PE classes help girls maintain the kinesthetic and inner sense of their bodies and are geared towards all body types. Use math classes to figure out what happens when somebody loses 10 lbs and gains it back with 10% more. How much do they gain after 5 diets?

Decide on girls or boys only or on mixed classes: Although this manual was written for girls, you can also use the information and adapt the activities for use with boys or for use with mixed groups. Mixed groups are appropriate before girls reach puberty as long as you recognize gender differences and adapt your lessons so that they honor the different ways in which girls and boys learn.

Once girls reach puberty, you can address emotionally neutral topics such as metabolism, genetics, healthy eating, and media literacy and awareness in mixed groups. Sometimes you can even teach communication skills, conflict resolution and bullying strategies—depending on the class.

It is strongly advised that you separate the girls from the boys when you address the changes in girls' bodies, the pressures on them to be kind and nice and accommodating, when you want to honor female gender culture and to encourage girls to be aware of their grungies and to talk about what's underneath. Girls enter puberty before boys do and are self-conscious about their bodies. Frequently they are teased. Most girls won't talk about anything personal or share anything that makes them vulnerable if there is one boy present. (Think about how we as adult women quickly change topics and our style of communication when a man joins our group.) Teaching girls separately allows us to create a climate of safety. It gives us the opportunity to model healthy relationships with girls, validate female culture, schmooze with girls and teach them how to support each other.

Making Presentations Meaningful

Presentations are mini-lessons with humor. While you can apply the above guidelines for classroom lessons, some of the procedures are going to be different.

Remember the *GOLDEN RULES OF PREVENTION***:** Whenever I am asked to do presentations I talk about the changes in girls' bodies and the changes in their lives and what happens to girls in the process of growing up. I talk about why girls feel fat and what that means and why some girls are fat. I then teach the audience about the grungies. If time permits, I include an activity that reinforces what I am trying to teach or strategies the audience can use.

Leave something for next time: We all have a tendency to give too much information. It might be because presentations are often one-shot events and we feel we must tell the audience everything we know. When we do this we talk too fast and are too formal and impersonal. The audience tunes us out. Too much information can overwhelm people and make them feel a lack of confidence to try out the skills we have taught.

Avoid 'Fuzzy Brain Syndrome': Regardless of their age, most people have an attention span of roughly 20 minutes. This gives you enough time to teach only one or two concepts. The rest of the time is spent reinforcing what you want your audience to learn.

Personalize the information: Presentations are mini-performances. In order to keep the audience engaged, you need to present the information in a way that makes it easy for them to relate to. Tell stories to illustrate your point. Give real life examples. Selectively share yourself. Use humor. A good presentation should be fun!

Give them something to take home: People always feel satisfied if there is something they can take home and practice. Teach them about the grungies. Provide strategies for whatever learning that you want to reinforce. Have them repeat an affirmation.

Avoid 'Numb Bum': There is only so long that people can sit and listen, regardless of how stimulating you are. Try to include an activity or take a break and let people move around. The best learning often comes from schmoozing with the other participants.

Frame your presentation in the context of their lives: Naming people's fears and concerns gives them a sense you understand them. It makes them feel validated. It gives them language with which to talk about their fears and concerns and opens the door for discussion.

Cultivate questions: Most girls and women are reluctant to ask questions in a large group or in a mixed group. When I do large presentations, I give each person an index card and pencil when they come in. I tell them they cannot fail asking questions, that there is no "dumb" question and that their questions are important because every time someone asks a question, there are usually about 10 other people who thought of roughly the same thing. I usually take a break in the presentation and ask the audience to write down their questions and place them in a basket. Because the questions are anonymous, people feel free to voice their concerns. This is a very valuable part of the presentation because it gives people the opportunity to ask what they really would like to know and because they can learn from each other.

SAMPLE PRESENTATIONS ON THE GRUNGIES

Elementary/Middle School (grades 5–7)

Best Friend: I like to engage an audience before I start my presentation. I usually ask girls to think about their best friend and tell me what makes that person their best friend. I repeat all the qualities they name and then bring to their attention that nobody said they chose their best friend because she was thin. I tell them, "Imagine choosing Jessica because she was thin. Imagine going over to Jessica's house and watching Jessica's thinness. It's so stimulating…" After the laughter subsides, I add "Isn't it interesting we never value ourselves for the same qualities we value in others?"

Introduce grungies: I ask girls how many of them have felt fat, ugly or stupid in the last week. I describe what a grungie is.

How grungies develop: Talk about the changes in girls' bodies…

- ➢ How your hips widen at a time when all the images around you tell you to be thin.
- ➢ How fat is necessary for menstruation.
- ➢ Getting your period and the effect of hormones.
- ➢ How girls are hungry but are afraid to eat.
- ➢ Talk about the changes in girls' lives.
- ➢ The pressure to be kind and nice and therefore the fear of hurting others.
- ➢ How girls learn to withhold their feelings and opinions.
- ➢ How girls worry about what other people think about them.

Explain how girls give themselves grungies when they can't talk about what is real.

- ➢ Give examples of grungies and stories that are underneath.
- ➢ Have girls think of a time when they felt fat. Have them be curious about what they were thinking, feeling at the time.

Do a *DEAD FLOWER CEREMONY*—I use this to encourage self-expression (see page 61). You can also use the strategies in *Celebrate Who You Are* on page 77.

Include a physical activity: Because most girls don't equate self-esteem with being active, I encourage discussion about how we feel good about ourselves when we use our bodies. Use the *Girlpower Rap* on page 129 or write your own and have the girls put movement to it.

GIRLPOWER RAP

I may be short I may be tall

I may be big, I may be small

Sometimes I'm happy, Sometimes I'm sad

Sometimes I'm loving, Sometimes I'm mad

Sometimes I'm right, Sometimes I'm wrong

My heart is open and my body is strong

I'm not a fragile flower

I'M A GIRL WITH GIRLPOWER!!

© 2003, Sandra Friedman, Salal Communications Ltd., www.salal.com

Middle/Secondary School (grades 7–9)

This is the most vulnerable time for girls. Many girls have already begun to experiment with dieting as they make the transition into high school. Your efforts at this time should include stopping behaviors before they can develop into eating disorders. This sample presentation builds on the previous one.

Best Friend: begin with the Best Friend

Introduce grungies: (see pages 55-61) Ask these girls how many of them have felt fat, ugly or stupid in the last week. What else do they tell themselves to make themselves feel badly? Describe grungies:

- How grungies develop: Talk about the changes in girls' bodies:
- How fat is necessary for menstruation.
- Getting your period and the effects of hormones.
- How girls are hungry but are afraid to eat.
- Talk about the pressure that girls put on each other about what they are eating and how they look.
- Talk about the need to be perfect and what that means.

Talk about the changes in girls' lives.

➤ The pressure to be kind and nice and the fear of hurting someone else.

➤ How girls learn to withhold their feelings and opinions.

➤ How girls worry about what other people think about them, especially boys.

➤How girls lose their sense of self. (see *Bottle of Beans* on page 131).

Explain that when girls can't talk about what is real, they give themselves grungies. Help girls practice identifying grungies. You can do this in pairs or groups of three.

Do a *DEAD FLOWER CEREMONY*—use this to encourage self-expression.

Talk about how we come in all shapes and sizes and what happens when we diet. Let girls know we can be fat and healthy if we are physically active. Talk about the benefits of physical activity. Ask girls how they can be physically active and what barriers stop them from doing so. Encourage them to begin with small steps.

Explain that eating disorders are coping mechanisms that begin when girls feel fat all the time and when their behavior around food is out of control. Let girls know that when this happens they need to talk to someone because it is very difficult to deal with this alone.

Close with an *AFFIRMATION*:

AFFIRMATION

I only have one body.
I will honor it.

I only have one life.
I will value it.

Not tomorrow.
Not when I get thin.

But NOW!

TEACHING SENSE-OF-SELF

BOTTLE OF BEANS

Materials: plastic dishwashing detergent bottle (girl-shaped)
enough beans to fill the container
large bowl

Before girls reach puberty they are full of themselves—'full of beans.' They haven't yet been affected by gender socialization so they speak their minds, stand up for themselves, are active, creative and are still connected to us. Once girls go through adolescence, the pressure on them to be kind and nice and hold back their opinions and feelings causes them to disconnect from themselves, to please other people and to look outward for definition. In the process, they 'lose their beans'—their sense-of-self. The Bottle of Beans helps girls, their parents and professionals understand how girls lose their sense of self and how they can get it back.

➢ Fill the bottle full of beans.

➢ Talk about how 'full of beans' means being 'full of yourself' and expressing your feelings and ideas.

➢ Pass the container around and have everyone feel the weight and sturdiness of the bottle when it is full. That is the same solidity that girls experience when they feel connected to themselves.

➢ Tell participants they lose their beans (or their sense-of-self) every time they seek to please others, worry about what others think about them, and focus on how they look or on anything external.

➢ Give your own examples and ask everyone for their examples of how you lose your beans. (e.g. "Am I good enough? What do you think of me?") For each example, pour some beans into the bowl.

➢ When the bottle is near empty, pass it around again. Have everyone note how light it is, how it lacks substance and how easy it is to knock over.

➢ Have everyone give examples of 'I' statements. Have them talk about their opinions, feelings and ideas. Each time put beans back into the bottle to show how you build or strengthen the sense-of-self.

Incorporate the 'full of beans' metaphor into your practice.

131.

HOLDING A GIRLS' DAY

In the past few years I have participated in numerous girls' day conferences—the most popular being those for grade seven. Some have been very exciting and empowering while others felt like just another day at school. Because I truly believe girls benefit from days that are dedicated just to them, I have included suggestions for holding a girls' day in your school or community.

Goals: To celebrate being female and female culture
To nurture *girlpower*
To teach the basic elements of prevention

Who Attends: Try to keep the day limited to one grade. Even one year makes a difference in the dynamics around girls, My preference would be grade seven because it can be a difficult time for girls who are about to make (or have just made) the transition to middle or secondary school. In small communities, you might have to combine grades six and seven or seven and eight—but if you do so, make sure some of the activities that you offer are separate for each grade.

Build Partnerships: Make the day a community event. Involve the women's center, parks and recreation, Girl Guides, Scouts and other organizations that are involved with girls. Making the day a community event offers girls perspectives and personalities different from their teachers'. It provides role models and reinforces prevention as a community responsibility.

Involve Peer Counselors: Girls learn best from other girls. Peer counselors can help facilitate groups. They can then help younger girls make the transition to a new school. Using peer counselors also comes with an ulterior motive—they learn the same prevention skills that the younger girls do.

Bring in Outside Resource People: This increases the 'bank' of role models girls are exposed to. Someone new also has a better chance of being heard because she is a new face and personality. Local celebrities who are young women (athletes, DJs, newsreaders, etc.) can really galvanize the room.

Involve Girls in Every Stage of Planning and Implementation: This helps them develop leadership skills. It also helps them own the event. Girls can help select the topics. They can interview resource people and introduce and thank them. They can be involved with setting up the location and with the tasks that are necessary to make the day go smoothly.

Vary Your Activities: Make sure you have both large and small group activities. The kind of learning that takes place in each situation is different.

Use a Catchy Title: Stay away from concepts like body image and self-esteem. Adults like them but girls tune them out.

Remember the *GOLDEN RULES OF PREVENTION:* Include an activity that deals with body issues and one that deals with self issues.

Program Suggestions:

➤ Teach girls about the grungies. Break them into small groups. Have the group role play one person's grungie and a different way of responding to what is going on.

➤ Use the *DEAD FLOWER CEREMONY.*

➤ Have girls make a collage that shows how they see themselves, what they value about themselves and what they think is important to them.

➤ Have girls celebrate the women in their lives. Make a collage about them.

➤ Include a physical activity. Belly dancing encourages girls with different body types and skill levels to get involved. Encourage girls to put movements to the Girlpower Rap on page 129. Include a lot of stretching and movement. Help girls equate physical activity with self-esteem.

➤ Teach girls self-defense. It's a great way for them to use their bodies.

➤ Teach girls assertiveness training.

➤ Have someone talk about sexual health.

➤ Have someone talk about the history of the community and the role of the women and girls in it.

➤ Bring in a variety of role models from different occupations and professions. Station them in different locations. Have small groups of girls move from one role model to another. This gives them the opportunity to ask questions in small groups.

➤ Bring in a hairdresser and have her give girls hair cuts.

➤ Teach relaxation techniques.

Above all, make sure that you have good food and that the day is fun. There is no law that says that girls can't learn if they are having a good time!

FACILITATING GROUPS

Peer groups are very important to girls who measure themselves against the way others see them. They are a major influence in shaping the attitudes and behaviors of girls around food, weight and body shape. Thus the more activities conducted with peer groups and the more these groups work together to encourage healthy self-expression and body attitudes, the more powerful a program can be in bringing about change in both the individual and their groups.[1]

The peer group gives girls an opportunity to test their opinions, feelings and attitudes against those of other girls and to decide which of their parental and societal values they will accept or reject. It also provides girls with emotional security. If you want to change behavior, challenge societal influences and teach skills the best way to do this in through a peer group where girls can learn the same skills and support each other, and where they all adopt the same belief system.

➤ Groups help girls reinforce their female culture through the intimacy and connection that comes from sharing feelings and experiences.

➤ Groups let girls know they are not alone in how they feel and that their feelings are normal.

➤ Groups validate girls' feelings. They let them know they have a right to the way they feel.

➤ Groups provide a societal and gender context for girls so they understand why they feel the way they do.

➤ Groups teach girls to support one another.

➤ Groups are suited for interactive and participatory activities because they are small and they provide girls with a safe place to try out new behavior.

Format of Groups

The ideal group is between six and eight participants because that is the size where girls feel safe. Groups can be larger if there is a co-facilitator and if there is the opportunity to break into smaller groups.

---

[1] Susan J. Paxton. "Peer Relations, Body Image and Disordered Eating in Adolescent Girls: Implications for Prevention," in Niva Piran, Michael P. Levine & Catherine Steiner-Adair, eds. *Preventing Eating Disorders: A Handbook of Interventions and Special Challenges.* Philadelphia: Francis and Taylor, 1999

> Groups should include between ten and twelve sessions. This gives girls enough time to learn, practice and reinforce new skills and behaviors.

> Groups should be on average one and one-half hours long. If the group is too short it is hard to ensure everyone gets a chance to speak and to feel heard. If the group is too long, we lose the interest and attention of the girls.

> Groups can be held on a drop-in basis or on a regular basis with fixed attendance. Drop-in groups allow girls to miss sessions because of other demands on their time and to bring their friends after they have tried out the group first. Fixed groups provide more safety and stability to the group process. They also allow facilitators to more easily include girls who they consider to be high risk.

Core Structure of the Group[1]

> Groups should operate according to a core structure that is repeated each week. The structure that is described here is the *JUST FOR GIRLS* structure. You can use it as is, or adapt it to fit your own needs and the needs of the girls. *JUST FOR GIRLS* is a group discussion program for girls that addresses the challenges that they face during and following the developmental stage of early adolescence. It teaches girls about the grungies and encourages them to express the stories that lie underneath. In doing so it helps girls find ways to express their responses to a challenging environment other than through the language of fat (see RESOURCES).

> The facilitator begins each group by sharing a little of who she is. It is important that women who facilitate groups for girls are willing to bring their personal selves into their professional lives. The greatest gift that we give to girls is our willingness to model healthy female relationships by engaging honestly with them, by letting them know what we think and feel and by sharing our own experiences of the world.

> At the beginning of each session the facilitator describes the purpose of the group and lets the girls know what is expected of them. She assures that nobody can fail—there is no right or wrong answer or way to do an activity. She also points out how girls compare themselves critically with one another and asks them to be aware of this. This creates an atmosphere of safety.

> The girls are reassured they have complete confidentiality unless they are in situations where they are in danger. This means what they say will not be repeated to their parents or teachers without their permission and nobody will talk about them when they leave the room.

---

[1] Sandra Friedman. *Just For Girls*. Vancouver: Salal Books, 1999, 2003 (2nd edition)

- Each week the girls are asked to remember a time the previous week when they were 'hit by a grungie.' That is, when they felt or told themselves that they were fat, ugly or stupid, etc. They are asked to talk about what else was happening to them at that particular time. They are encouraged to tell the story again—but this time without the grungie and expressing the feelings that are underneath.

- The facilitator responds to each girl. She validates her experiences and feelings and provides her with a context that is framed in female culture and socialization. In doing so she lets the girl know she is not alone in how she feels and she has a right to feel the way she does.

- The custom of the Talking Stick has been borrowed from the First Nations (American Indian) people and has been adapted for use by the group. As the Talking Stick is passed around the group, only the person holding it may speak. The Talking Stick is used to ensure each girl has an opportunity to speak uninterrupted and to be listened to.

- Topics are introduced that address the developmental issues of the age group involved. In order to implement the GOLDEN RULES OF *PREVENTION*, you might spend one session talking about puberty and the changes in girls' bodies. A follow-up session might be spent answering their questions. Encourage girls to write their questions on slips of paper and put them into an envelope. You can then spend another session talking about the pressures girls feel to be kind and nice, and then practice being assertive and saying no. Activities encourage self-expression, address girls' concerns, build communication skills and help girls accept their natural bodies. (***JUST FOR GIRLS*** has a section that addresses the issues and concerns to girls and provides you with session plans you can use, and activities you can do.)

- In working with girls in a relational way, the facilitator must ensure she validates their own experiences as source of information and knowledge and all activities and information are set in the context of their lives and experiences. In facilitating groups care must be taken to continuously find a balance between the process that is at the heart of the program and the structure that allows for the development of skills. Facilitators also need to be prepared to put their plans aside in order to meet the immediate needs of the girls.

- At the close of each session, each girl is encouraged to say something positive about herself, about her abilities, or about what makes her interesting as a person.

INTERVENTION

Eating disorder prevention (also known as *primary* prevention) is about promoting and sustaining healthy development and nurturing *girlpower* as it already exists. It targets girls of elementary and middle school ages and addresses the challenges they face as they make the transition from childhood through adolescence. Because it occurs before the fact, prevention has very little to do with eating disorders or with the behaviors associated with them.

Intervention (also known as *secondary* prevention or early intervention) is about stopping behaviors before they escalate into full-blown eating disorders, and restoring the *girlpower* that is in the process of deterioration. It is targeted mainly at girls in middle and secondary school—girls with disordered eating who are just beginning to experiment with dieting, fasting, bingeing, purging and excessive exercise.

INTERVENTION INVOLVES...

Helping girls stop the behaviors.
> Addressing the changes in girls' bodies and their body issues.
> Addressing the changes in girls' lives and their self issues.

Helping girls identify and address the issues that lie underneath the behaviors.
> Identifying and addressing personal and societal stressors.

Addressing girls' issues in the context of their experiences and lives and in the context of the society in which we live.
> Understanding female development
> Understanding developmental/life stage issues

Referring to appropriate sources when girls are at medical risk and/or when treatment is necessary.

Even the mention of eating disorders is enough to scare most people—regardless of how much training they have in other areas. The participants in my workshops on intervention describe a common reaction to intervening with someone who they think is at risk: while they want to help that person, visions of starving girls begin to dance around in their heads. They don't know where to begin. They are afraid whatever they say will make her worse; that she will collapse right in front of them and that it will be their fault. If only they had four more courses and another degree they would be better able to do this work.

The chapter on eating disorders provided you with basic information and an understanding of the disorders themselves. This chapter will help you demystify eating disorders so you can understand the dynamics and address the triggers. It will help you look beyond the disorder to see the girl instead of just her behaviors. It will provide you with basic counseling skills to use with girls who are experimenting with disordered eating behaviors so that they can address what lies underneath.

Building Confidence

The first step in intervention is building our confidence in ourselves. In our fear of doing something wrong or trying something new we often discount our own abilities and competence. Once we can recognize that we all have varying degrees of skill we can try to intervene from a position of curiosity instead of self-doubt and self-consciousness.

Know and respect where you are on the continuum. Counseling skills exist on a continuum of experience which ranges from people who are just beginning to learn and implement these skills to those who are experienced in counseling in other areas and are adding disordered eating/eating disorders to their practice. Regardless of our level of skill and experience we all have something valuable to contribute. There is no perfect counselor just as there is no perfect treatment model.

Acknowledge the skills and competence you bring to the situation even though you may not be an 'eating disorder' specialist. Remind yourself of your ability to relate to girls, and of other situations where you have felt confident and competent. Allow yourself to be nervous. We are all unsure when we try something new.

Remember disordered eating/eating disorders are coping mechanisms that develop over a period of time. There is little you can say you or do that has such a great impact it will make the disordered eating worse for the girl—as long as you don't encourage weight loss, make her feel guilty for not 'getting better,' or make comments about her weight and shape other than expressing concern. Someone who is going to binge, purge, fast, restrict their food intake and/or exercise excessively will do so until she is ready and able to replace these behaviors with more healthy ways of coping.

Intervention is not so much about having the right techniques and things to do but about connection. Every girl has a story and every girl wants to feel heard. She wants to be reassured we know or can imagine what her experience or feelings are like for her. She also wants us to not judge her if our experiences and feelings are different from hers. Once you connect with and become curious about the girl and her story and take the emphasis off fixing her your performance anxiety will go away.

Regardless of your intentions or your level of skill, even you are not so powerful that you alone can fix girls' problems and make them all better. What you can do is connect to girls, help them become aware of and resolve their issues and teach them healthier ways of dealing with feelings and with situations in their lives.

THE GOLDEN RULE OF COUNSELING

I did not break it,

I cannot fix it,

I am not a plumber!

Don't work alone. Work with the family doctor to ensure the girl is not at medical risk. We can't always tell just be looking at her. If you are the only resource in your community (as is often the case in rural and remote areas) consult with the professionals at the eating disorder centre in your province or state. Asking for help and for reassurance is not a sign of weakness. It is a sign of strength. If there are no resources you can access or you don't know where to begin looking, contact the organizations listed in the *RESOURCE* section at the end of this book.

Recognize the Early Warning Signs

Before you continue on with this section you might want to reread the chapter on eating disorders to refresh your understanding of what the behaviors are about and what they mean to girls. Familiarize yourself with the early warning signs of disordered eating described on the next page so that you can recognize them when you see them. You don't need to memorize them but you do need to know where to look for reference.

EARLY WARNING SIGNS OF DISORDERED EATING

➤ Constantly 'feeling fat' and making comments about her weight.

➤ Fear of becoming fat.

➤ Dieting.

➤ Frequent measuring of body weight or muscle size.

➤ Weighing herself at least once a day.

➤ Obsessing about the calorie and fat content of food.

➤ Removing food groups from their diet (e.g. dairy, meat).

➤ Avoiding eating with others.

➤ Very low intake of food (average teen needs 2200-3000 calories daily).

➤ Becoming vegetarian.

➤ Skipping meals.

➤ Exercising excessively to lose weight.

➤ Feeling guilty and anxious when unable to exercise.

➤ Putting herself down and being overly sensitive to criticism.

➤ Experiencing mood swings and irritability.

➤ Dramatic weight fluctuations.

➤ Sleep disturbances.

➤ Low self-esteem and poor self image.

➤ Believing personal value comes from how you look or your weight.

➤ Constantly worrying about what other people think of her.

➤ Needing to be perfect in everything she does.

➤ Withdrawing from social activities with friends or family.

➤ Experiencing a loss or disruption of friendship.

➤ Experiencing a transition or a disruption in her/his life.

➤ Using steroids or steroid precursors to build muscle.

Warning Signs in Athletes

Many girls are participating in different sports today. Some of these girls will take their participation to an extreme—especially athletes who believe being thin will help their performance. Often an athlete considered a 'good athlete' and one at risk of developing an eating disorder show many of the same characteristics. We need to be able to recognize the signs of athletes at risk so we can intervene instead of praising these girls for their commitment, compliance and persistence.

The "Good" Athlete[2]

➢ Is willing to train and exercise harder and longer than her teammates.

➢ Performs through pain and injury.

➢ Is selflessly committed to her team.

➢ Complies completely with coaching instructions in order to please others.

➢ Accepts nothing less than perfection.

➢ Is willing to lose weight to improve performance.

The Athlete at Risk of Disordered Eating/Eating Disorders

➢ Is a perfectionist with high goals.

➢ Has a strong desire to please others.

➢ Bases her self worth on achievement and not performance.

➢ Is willing to tolerate pain and sacrifices herself to meet her goals.

➢ Is critical of herself and has high expectations in sport and life.

➢ Places emphasis on maintaining an "ideal body weight" or optimal body fat.

Pay Attention to the Context

Disordered eating behaviors occur in response to a trigger such as a feeling that is too scary to express or which the girl cannot identify, an event for which she has no language or does not feel safe talking about or a thought that is unacceptable to her self image. Understanding the context helps us identify the trigger and break the situation into manageable parts.

---

[2] Adapted from materials created by Dr. Ron Thompson and Dr. Roberta Trattner Sherman, International Academy of Eating Disorders Conference (2000) in "Disordered Eating and Athletes: The Facts," *Bodysense*   www.bodysense.ca

---

CONTEXT OF DISORDERED EATING/EATING DISORDERS
Societal Pressures
Developmental/Gender Issues
Problematic Life Experiences
Family Dynamics
Body Issues/Self Issues

Understand the Risks and Challenges of Each Stage of Development

Each stage of development poses challenges that must be worked through and risk factors that make girls vulnerable to disordered eating/eating disorders. During adolescence girls must also deal with their 'imaginary audience'—their heightened self-consciousness that people are watching them. This is also a time when girls' feelings can be very intense and they believe whatever they are feeling in the moment will never end.

Early Adolescence (around 11 to 13 years of age)

➤ Social, emotional and physical changes that occur during puberty.

➤ Early bloomers and late bloomers.

➤ Transition to high school.

➤ Changing dynamics of friendships—teasing, exclusion, secrets.

➤ Teasing.

➤ Problems with parents.

➤ School pressures.

➤ Boys and sexuality.

➤ Loss of aerobic capacity.

Middle Adolescence (around 14 to 16 years old)

➤ Increasing independence—how to achieve both autonomy and connection.

➤ Anxiety about friendships.

➤ Boys and sexuality.

➤ Pressure to achieve.

➤ Pressure to be perfect (i.e. thin and confident).

Later Adolescence (around 17-19 years old)

> Transition from high school to college or workplace.

> Leaving home.

> Internalization of male values.

> Pressures to achieve.

> Relationships and sexuality.

> Stressors in daily life.

Know Who Is At Risk

Knowing who is at risk can help you ask questions that can identify the triggers of disordered eating behaviors.

Girls at Risk of Developing Eating Disorders may...

> Mature early.

> Have low self-esteem.

> Lack intimate connections with others.

> Have experienced changes or loss in their major relationships.

> Have had problematic life experiences.

> Have been sexually or physically abused.

> Have parents who are chronically depressed.

> Have parents who abuse alcohol or drugs.

> Have families with rigid rules or with no boundaries.

> May be teased about their weight.

> Have mothers and friends who diet.

> Have fathers who make comments about their weight.

> Read magazines that emphasize thinness and dieting.

> Have a chronic illness.

> *Be* fat.

Understand the Psychological Characteristics

Girls with disordered eating often have certain psychological characteristics in the way that they experience and relate to the world. Knowing what these are will help you name them so that girls can recognize and address them.

> Girls often exhibit 'black and white' or 'all or nothing' thinking.

> Girls often use language that is global instead of being specific about what is happening right now.

> Girls have difficulty with limits and boundaries. They are terrified if they say no they will hurt the other person who will then reject them.

> Relationships are scary:

  • Girls fear losing themselves in their attempts to please others.

  • Girls are afraid of being dominated or of being overwhelmed.

> Girls have difficulty with feelings:

  • They believe that painful feelings will last forever, and they use food related behaviors to try to make the feelings go away.

  • They are afraid of being overwhelmed by their feelings.

  • They are afraid their feelings will overwhelm others.

> Girls have trouble asking for help. They believe they should resolve their eating disorders by themselves.

> Girls are caught between wanting to please their families by giving up their eating disorder and their shame about hurting them because of their own needs.

> Girls who have difficulty dealing with stress are often unable to tolerate anxiety. They use behaviors around food to make it go away.

> Girls often place unrealistic demands on themselves in order to gain the approval of others. No matter how well they do, they still think they have failed.

> Control is about being able to say 'yes' and 'no.' When girls can't do this directly, they feel powerless and find other ways of creating control (or order) in their lives.

APPLYING COUNSELING SKILLS

How you interact with girls, the questions you ask, the experiences you share and the dynamics between you will be influenced by your skills, interests and personality. No two people engage in counseling in the same way. In one intervention workshop a teacher who was role-playing a counseling situation stopped in mid sentence and said, "This is not how I interact with kids." Once she was able to deal with the situation in her way and with her own style, she was able to connect with the other person.

Develop a Relationship with the Girl

The most important part of any counseling situation is the relationship that you form with the girl. No matter how many degrees, years of experience and techniques you have nothing is going to happen if you can't form a connection with the girl.

Schmooze with her. Girls need us to validate their feelings and to connect with them. When I said this in one workshop, the psychiatric nurses gave a collective sigh of relief. They were so afraid of 'breaking' the girls on their ward that they distanced themselves from them. Once they learned the *GOLDEN RULE OF COUNSELING* and that they could just be themselves, they were able to connect with girls and validate their feelings around being in the hospital and being forced to eat.

Share yourself selectively (pages 35-37). We all remember painful moments from our own adolescence—the boys who dumped us, the pressure to do well in school, the fights we had with our parents, the ups and downs of our relationships. Sharing ourselves selectively gives girls permission and language to talk about issues that are painful and are of concern to them and acknowledge feelings that make them feel guilty. It lets them know they are not abnormal or alone in how they feel and builds and strengthens the connection that we have with them. Girls are not so afraid of opening up to us when they feel we understand them and we will share ourselves—and not judge them.

Instead of always asking her how or what she is feeling, describe the situation or stressor and the feelings you think she might be having. For example, you might say something like: "Sometimes girls try really hard but no matter how well they do they feel like a fraud, like someone else wrote the composition. Is that what's happening to you?" Or "Sometimes girls are so afraid of hurting someone else that they find it hard to tell the person how they feel. Is that what's happening to you?" This is important because girls are quick to discount their feelings and negate their experiences. Because the range of their feelings is narrow they often don't know what they are feeling or have the language with which to articulate it. However, when you provide her with language and permission to talk about different things, remember to continuously check out if what you are describing is in fact true for her so that you don't ascribe feelings to her.

Be curious about aspects of her life other than her eating disorder behavior. Any girl can be funny, bright, stubborn, talented and interested in different things. Girls with eating disorders deal with the same issues as other adolescent girls. We need to be able to see the girl instead of just the disorder.

Pay Attention to Yourself

Counseling someone is as much about you and your attitudes and reactions as it is about the girl you are working with. This doesn't mean you have to be perfect. It means you need to pay attention to what is going on with you at the same time that you are paying attention to what is going on with the girl.

If you begin to feel frustrated and angry it is probably because you are trying to stop the behaviors and the girl is not cooperating with you. Even though girls may want to 'get better' there is always an underlying conflict. On one hand they know the behaviors are harmful and they should stop. On the other hand nobody gives up a coping mechanism without replacing it with something else and this takes time and small steps.

If you begin to feel overwhelmed by what the girl is telling you it is because she is either telling her story in global terms and is using all or nothing language or she is talking about too many things. Help her (and yourself) focus on one specific situation and trigger.

If you are spacing out, or feeling anxious or bored, listening selectively or distancing your self from her story it may be because something in her story or mannerisms is triggering something painful for you. Be curious about what is behind your reaction Ask yourself what it is about her behavior or story you are having difficulty with.

If you are bored or the energy is either very low or dead, the girl is not 'present' and the connection is broken. Try to work with the feelings around a specific situation.

Don't forget the *Golden Rule of Counseling*. Until you develop your own style of counseling and confidence in what you are doing you may have to repeat it many times.

Remember that girls with disordered eating/eating disorders are heroes. It takes a tremendous amount of courage to face your fears, work through your preoccupation with food and weight and replace your coping mechanisms. It is also a very slow process.

In the Beginning

➤ Listen to her with openness and curiosity. When you are curious about what is going on for her and are not fixated on doing everything right you can stay with her energy and follow your instincts. Every girl has a story. She needs to be able to tell it. We need to be able to listen to it without always feeling that we have to fix it. Sometimes that's the best kind of counseling that we can do.

➢ Encourage her to become curious about the behaviors. When you place the emphasis on stopping the behaviors, girls may not come back to you because they think they have failed counseling. Let her know sometimes we need to continue doing what we are doing in order to learn about it. (I call it the 'detective' approach to counseling.) Assure her you will continue to see her even if she continues bingeing, purging, fasting, dieting, etc.

➢ Instead of describing someone as anorexic, bulimic or a compulsive eater, describe her as a girl *with* anorexia, bulimia or compulsive eating. The eating disorder is only one part of who she is.

➢ Avoid saying things such as "This is not you speaking. It is the anorexia," or "I'm not angry with you. I'm angry with your eating disorder." Girls can become cognitively impaired when their weight drops below the danger line and 'hear voices' that are a function of the anorexia telling them that they are fat and that they should not eat. However this is not true of most girls whose weight is still above the danger line—especially the girls you will be dealing with. Attributing their thoughts and feelings to the anorexia makes them feel discounted and unheard.

➢ Teach her there is no right or wrong even though feelings may seem irrational and unfair. Everybody has a right to what she feels.

➢ Encourage her to take little baby steps to resolve her issues. Let her know she can change their mind and not do what she said she would do. Let her know she cannot fail.

Follow the Intervention Process

➢ Intervention follows a process that is very similar to teaching girls about the grungies except in this case instead of placing the focus on feeling fat, it is placed on the disordered eating/eating disorder behaviors.

➢ Help her name and describe the behavior and to reframe it as a coping mechanism. Naming the behavior moves it from something that is happening to girls to something they can eventually change. It 'normalizes' it in the context of their disordered eating and helps girls move from shame to curiosity.

➢ Encourage her to remember the last time she felt fat, binged, purged and/or told herself not to eat and felt anxious. Help her become aware of when she feels small (anorexia) or too big (compulsive overeating). Girls often feel small or too big when they feel powerless.

➢ Use the same process for working with the grungies (pages 55-61). Ask her what she was thinking about at the time. You might ask 'What else was going on at that time? What were you thinking about? What were you feeling? Tell the story about your binge, purge, or fast without using those words but with dignity—by talking about the things that are real.

➢ Help her express her feelings and then help her explore and practice solutions. Remember that because most girls are afraid of doing something wrong, we need to focus on very tiny steps to reassure them they cannot fail.

➢ Validate her feelings and provide her with a context. It is important for girls to know they have the right to how they feel. Knowing why they feel the way they do takes away blame and shame and opens the door to curiosity.

➢ Even if she cannot discover what is underneath, it is important to help her make the connection between eating disorder behaviors and the thoughts and underlying feelings and experiences that trigger them. It is through understanding, articulating and sharing their knowledge of their own truths and their own personal experiences that girls are able to begin the process of change.

➢ Use the questions below only as a guide when you feel you are stuck or until you feel comfortable formulating your own. Take care you don't get so caught up in the questions you forget about the connection with the girl.

Questions You Might Ask

➢ How did you feel before and after the binge and or purge?

➢ When did you know you were going to binge/purge?

➢ What would have happened if you didn't?

➢ What was going on at that time? What were you thinking about?

➢ How much food is too much food?

➢ How does it feel when you take food into your body?

➢ How does it feel to reject it?

➢ When was the last time when you said to yourself "don't eat." What else was going on? What were you doing? What were you thinking?

➢ When was the last time you felt small or powerless? What else was going on? What were you doing? What were you thinking?

➢ If you didn't have to worry about being a nice person, what would you want to say to the person in your story?

Deal With Feelings

Girls experience conflict between what I like to describe as their *Sugar Plum Fairy* and *Zena the Amazon Warrior* personas. While all girls are socialized to hold back their feelings and opinions, girls with disordered eating/eating disorders experience a heightened fear of hurting someone else. Like the Sugar Plum Fairy they desire to be seen and to see themselves as 'nice.' They feel guilty about angry thoughts and even expressing them symbolically makes them feel guilty and mean. On the other hand, girls also have moments when they are like Zena the Amazon Warrior—ready to take on the world. Although they may be angry, their anger is reactive. Neither persona allows girls to acknowledge their feeling and express them directly to another person.

Girls need a lot of practice recognizing and symbolically expressing feelings such as anger hurt, disappointment and insecurity. Use the communication skills and exercises (on pages 62 to 68) to help girls recognize and express their feelings.

➢ Remind her that being angry with yourself is learned behavior. I tell girls while my cat Theodora will whap you if you touch her the wrong way, I've never seen her scratching herself and meowing 'bad cat.' Ask her what she would want to say to the person in her story if she didn't have to worry about being a nice person. Encourage her to express her anger symbolically and directly instead of turning it against herself. She can do this:

- With the *DEAD FLOWER* CEREMONY (page 61).

- By giving *roses* and *onions* to the person that she is having difficulty with. Girls can speak to someone symbolically by imagining the person is in their imagination, in the room, on a spot on the floor or on a chair, etc. Speaking to someone symbolically may not change the situation but it allows girls to express the feelings instead of keeping them inside. Girls must use their voice and speak directly to the person— otherwise the thoughts will go around and around in their heads and turn into grungies and then into triggers for disordered eating/eating disorder behaviors.

➢ Have her name a person she is having difficulty with. Have her think of two things that draw her to that person and two things that make her move away. Encourage her to use the feedback skills to tell the person how her/his behavior makes her feel. Avoid using terms such as 'good things' and 'bad things.' Do the same exercise about a friend or a potential romantic interest. This helps girls recognize, validate and hone their perception skills. It also helps them realize not everything is about them and they are not to blame for difficulties that arise in relationships or if the other person is not interested in them.

➢ Remind her every time she expresses her feelings directly she moves the focus away from the other person or from outside back to herself. This helps her feel in control because she is in not dependent on the other person for what she feels.

➢ Help her deal with other peoples' feelings. Teach her how two people may have very different feelings about the same event or interaction and that each person's feelings are valid. When our friends feel hurt, we can't just step into their experience and take their feelings away. We can, however, let the other person know that we can see how they feel even though we feel differently.

Challenge Beliefs

Help girls become aware of and examine their negative beliefs or 'hot thoughts.' Hot thoughts are automatic thoughts and assumptions such as their negative voice, their 'shoulds,' their beliefs about what other people think about them, their global thinking in terms of never and always and their beliefs about food, eating, and body shape and size.

For example: If I eat this I will get fat.

If I tell Anna that I am angry she will reject me.

If Brian doesn't ask me out it is because I am ugly.

➢ Have girls list the evidence that supports the 'hot thought.'

➢ Have girls list the evidence that does not support the 'hot thought.'

➢ Have girls replace the 'hot thought' with a balanced, realistic thought.

WHAT YOU THINK ABOUT, YOU BRING ABOUT

Notice your THOUGHTS > they become FEELINGS

Notice your feelings > they become WORDS

Notice your words > they become ACTIONS

Notice your actions > they become HABITS

Notice your habits > they become CHARACTER

Notice your character > it becomes your DESTINY

WHAT YOU THINK ABOUT, YOU BRING ABOUT
(*NEGATIVE THOUGHT:* You Failed a Test)

Notice your THOUGHTS > they become FEELINGS
(If you think "I'm a failure", you feel sad, no control, stupid)

Notice your feelings > they become WORDS
(you say "what's wrong with me?", "I'll never do it right")

Notice your words > they become ACTIONS
(you give up, don't try)

Notice your actions > they become HABITS
(you become afraid to try new things for fear of failure)

Notice your habits > they become CHARACTER
(you have low self-worth and a negative attitude about your abilties)

Notice your character > it becomes your DESTINY
(now…YOUR DESTINY IS LIMITED)

from A QUEST FOR HEALTH, Sheena's Place   www.sheenasplace.org

Focus on a Specific Issue

Girls have little difficulty identifying an issue that is of concern to them when their energy about this issue is close to the surface. Sometimes, however, girls don't have or are not aware of a specific issue they are dealing with or they have so many issues they feel overwhelmed. Focusing is a good way to help girls find a place to begin.

➤ Have her put her feet firmly on the ground, close her eyes and center. (Do the exercise on page 115-116 but leave out the visualization.) Have her imagine that she is creating a space around herself. She can be in a bubble or draw a boundary around herself in her imagination.

➤ Ask her to keep her eyes closed and her say to herself silently "I would be a happy and relaxed person right now if I didn't have to deal with…" Have her use her imagination to put all the things she comes up with outside her space.

➤ Tell her to let you know when she has finished putting things outside her space. Give her a few minutes to do this and then check to see if she is stuck. If she is having difficulty, suggest that these things can be people, events, feelings. Let her know there is no right or wrong and that if she did the same exercise tomorrow, she might do it

151.

differently. If she is worrying about getting rid of things, reassure her she can take them all back at the end of the exercise.

➤ Ask her to select only one thing that she has put outside her space and to tell you what it is. Again, reassure her there is no right or wrong in what she selects. Explore this issue with her.

Deal with Anxiety and Fear

➤ Have her put her feet firmly on the ground, close her eyes and center. Have her talk about everything she is thinking about even it if doesn't make sense to her. Free association (or what seems like verbal purging) often helps identify where the anxiety is most intense. Once you have found what is making her anxious you can begin to explore it.

➤ Help her move from the global to the specific. Have her reduce her feelings and situations to tiny, manageable bits by being as specific as possible. Girls with disordered eating/eating disorders often use language that is black or white, or all or nothing. They are either fat or thin. Situations are always and never. They use global words such as my 'body image', 'my self-esteem', 'my life,' etc. I call global language 'garbage can language' because it doesn't mean anything specific and is so removed from girls' actual experiences there is no starting point for them to deal with the stressor. This makes them feel overwhelmed and anxious.

➤ Help her name her 'catastrophic expectation' or the worst thing that could happen about the situation you are focusing on. Explore evidence that supports this will happen and evidence that it won't. Help her negotiate a 'bottom line' or action or boundary to help her take back her power and feel in control. For example, you are going to a party and the catastrophic expectation is that nobody will talk to you. Bottom line: you will stay 15 minutes. If you are not having fun you will leave. You can decide to stay another 15 minutes and renegotiate the situation. You can do this every 15 minutes.

➤ Have her list her 'shoulds.' I tell girls that 'shoulds' are like tapes we automatically respond it. For example, if I activate a tape recorder with someone yelling "There's a fire" if they don't see that it's a tape they will most likely run outside the room. If they see me activate the tape recorder inside the office, they won't respond to the tape. Help girls become aware of where the 'shoulds came from and how realistic they are. Talk about what they can do to not respond to them.

➤ Draw or visualize a "fear thermometer." Ask her to rate her fear and/or anxiety in a specific moment or when talking about a specific event. Use the breathing and muscle relaxation techniques in on pages 116-117. Have her rate the fear again. Often when girls feel afraid or anxious they look for an instant solution and panic when they don't have one. This intensifies the anxiety. It's important for them to learn how to manage the fear in tiny baby steps.

Prioritize Issues

➤ Help her prioritize her issues by asking her what is the most distressing of all the things she has talked about. Address just that one issue. Adolescent girls experience things intensely. They think that whatever they are feeling in the moment will last forever. They believe that all issues are of equal value. You can begin by drawing a *STRESS TREE* (see page 117) and have her rank her issues as long-term or short-term and in a hierarchy of importance. Talk about what she can control and what they can't. Which of the items on the list can she let go of?

➤ After she has expressed her feelings, help her explore solutions to her stressors.

• Have her choose one stressor and be as specific as she can.

• Ask her how she has resolved situations before.

• Ask her to describe the strengths she has that have allowed her to feel good about resolving a situation.

• Tell her to imagine when she wakes up tomorrow the problem will be gone. Ask her what will be different. (This helps girls think beyond the problem.)

• Ask her to rate her problem/issue on a scale of 1 to 10 (where 1 is 'really bothering me' and 10 is 'resolved'). Ask her what would need to be different for her to move up one number on that scale?

When She is An Athlete

➤ Let her know her disordered eating behaviors will not necessarily prevent her from participating in her sport if she is not in medical danger.

➤ Help her establish boundaries and limits on her participation.

➤ Watch for disordered eating attitudes and behaviors spreading among other athletes. If someone is naturally thin and is performing well girls may believe they need to be thin in order to do well. Be aware that girls not only compete with others in sport. They compete with each other for thinness.

Be Kind To Yourself

Be kind to yourself. It's easy for us to pick up other girls' anxiety and panic and feel that we have to fix them. Yet we are not the driver but the tour guide. Girls move according to their own readiness and follow their own process. Change can often take a long time. Respect your own skills and abilities. In the end what matters most is not your bag of techniques and meaningful questions but the relationship that you have with the girl.

SHINE YOUR OWN LIGHT

Imagine that we all have a flashlight built right into our head. We become blinded by other peoples' lights whenever we look outside of ourselves for direction (as girls do when they look to others for definition or worry too much about what others think). This makes it difficult for us to see our own way.

We need to focus on our own lights. We can do that by stepping back and moving away from other people's lights. This will allow us to figure out what we are feeling and thinking and what we want.

RESOURCES

PUBLICATIONS

Anti-Diets and Size Acceptance

Am I Fat? Helping Young Children Accept Differences in Body Size.
J. Ikeda & P. Naworski. Santa Cruz, CA: ETR Associates, 1992

Big Fat Lies: The Truth about Your Weight and Your Health. (Updated edition)
Glenn A. Gaesser, PhD. Carlsbad, CA: Gurze Books, 2003

Healthy Weight Journal. Frances Berg, editor
Contact: B.C. Decker, Inc.
P.O. Box 785
Lewiston, NY   14092-0785
☎ 1-800-568-7281   🖷 1-905-522-7839
www.bcdecker.com   info@bcdecker.com

Making Peace with Food: Freeing Yourself from the Diet/Weight Obsession.
Susan Kano. New York, NY: HarperCollins, 1989

No Weigh—a non-dieting program for use with teenagers
HUGS International
Box 102A, RR3
Portage La Prairie, MB   R1N 3A3
☎ 1-800-565-4847   www.hugs.com

When Women Stop Hating Their Bodies: Freeing Yourself from Food and Weight Obsession.
Jane R. Hirschmann & Carol H. Munter. New York, NY: Fawcett Columbine/Ballantine
Books, 1995

Bodies

Amazing Schemes Within Your Genes and *DNA is Here to Stay.* Fran Balkwill and Mic
Rolph. Minnesota: Carolrhoda Books Inc., 1994   **Good book for girls**

Body Outlaws: Young Women Write About Body Image and Identity.
Edited by Ophira Edut. Seal Press, 2000

Body Talk: The Straight Facts on Fitness, Nutrition & Feeling Great About Yourself.
Ann Douglas & Julie Douglas. Toronto: Maple Tree Press, 2002   **Good book for girls**

Body Wars: Making Peace with Women's Bodies, An Activist's Guide.
Margo Maine, PhD. Carlsbad, CA: Gurze Books, 2000
Excellent information and resources including lists of media addresses.

The Cartoon Guide to Genetics.
Larry Gonick and Mark Wheelis. New York: Harper Collins, 1991 **Good book for girls**

Real Gorgeous: The truth about body and beauty. Kaz Cooke. New York, NY: Norton, 1995
Good information presented with lots of humor.

200 Ways to Love the Body You Have.
M. G. Hutchinson. Trumansburg, NY: Crossing Press, 1999

Boys

Real Boys: Rescuing Our Sons from the Myths of Boyhood.
William Pollack. New York, NY: Random House, 1998

The Wonder of Boys: What Parents, Mentors and Educators Can Do to Shape Boys into Exceptional Men. Michael Gurian. New York, NY: Jeremy P. Tarcher/Putnam, 1996

The Brain

Brain Sex: The Real Differences Between Men and Women.
Anne Moir & David Jessel. New York, NY: Dell Publishing, 1989

Sex on the Brain: The Biological Differences Between Men and Women.
Deborah Blum. New York, NY: Viking, 1997

Bullying

Battling the School-Yard Bully: How to Raise an Assertive Child in an Aggressive World.
Kim Zarzour. Toronto, ON: HarperCollins, 2000   (US edition: Firefly, 2000)

Focus on Bullying: A Prevention Program for Elementary School Communities.
British Columbia Ministry of Education & Ministry of the Attorney General.
Excellent material for developing a comprehensive, collaborative program.
Contact: BC Safe School Centre
    5325 Kincaid Street
    Burnaby, BC V5G 1W2
    ☎ 604-660-7233 1-888-224-SAFE-7233 🖨 604-664-8382
    www.safeschools.gov.bc.ca

Take Action Against Bullying. Gesele Lajoie, Alyson McLellan, Cindi Seddon. 1997
Contact: Bully B'Ware Productions
    1421 King Albert Avenue
    Coquitlam, BC V3J 1Y3
    ☎ and 🖨 604-936-8000   1-800-55BULLY

Communication/Conflict Resolution

Peer Mediation: Conflict Resolution in Schools (Program Guide and Student Manual)
Fred Schrumpf, Donna Crawford & Richard Bodine. Research Press, 1996

Viewpoints: A Guide to Conflict Resolution and Decision Making for Adolescents and *Teachers' Guide to Viewpoints.* Nancy G. Guerra, Ann Moore & Ronald Slaby. Research Press, 1995

Eating Disorders

The Adonis Complex: The Social Crisis of Male Body Obsession. Harrison G. Pope, Jr., MD, Katharine A. Phillips, MD, Roberto Olivardia, MD, Free Press, 2000

Anorexia's Fallen Angel. Barbara McClintock, Toronto: HarperCollins, 2002
(For those of you who keep asking about the Montreux Clinic in Victoria)

Consuming Passions: Feminist Approaches to Weight Preoccupation and Eating Disorders. Catrina Brown & Karin Jasper, editors. Toronto, ON: Second Story Press, 1993

Coping with Eating Disorders
Barbara Moe. New York, NY: Rosen Publishing Group, 1991

The Eating Disorder Sourcebook: A Comprehensive Guide to the Causes, Treatment and Prevention of Eating Disorders. Carolyn Costin, M.A., M.Ed, M.F.C.C., Los Angeles: Lowell House, 1997

Feminist Perspectives on Eating Disorders. Patricia Fallon, Melanie Katzman & Susan Wooley, editors. New York, NY: Guilford Press, 1994

Making Weight: Men's Conflicts with Food, Weight, Shape and Appearance. Arnold Anderson, MD, Leigh Cohn, MAT, Thomas Holbrook, MD, Gurze Books, 2000

Surviving an Eating Disorder: Strategies for Families and Friends. Michelle Siegel, Judith Brisman & Margot Weinshel. New York, NY: Harper Perennial, 1988

When Your Child Has An Eating Disorder: A Step-by-Step Workbook. Abigail H. Natenshon. San Francisco: Jossey-Bass Publishers, 1999

Eating Disorder Prevention/Intervention

Body Thieves: Help Girls Reclaim Their Natural Bodies and Become Physically Active. Sandra Friedman, Vancouver: Salal Books, 2002

Every Body is a Some BODY: Facilitator's Guide.
Andrea Seaver, Gail McVey, Yvonne Fullerton, Lorna Stratton
Designed for elementary and high school. Provides information and strategies on ways to promote positive body image among teen girls. Cost is $32 which includes shipping.
Contact: Body Image Coalition of Peel
            attn: Brenda Jones
            Peel Health
            180B Sandalwood Pkwy East, Suite 200
            Brampton ON   L6Z 4N1   ☎ 905-791-7800 (ext: 7665)

Healthy Body Image: Teaching Kids to Eat and Love their Bodies Too! Kathy J. Kater.
A comprehensive resource manual with introductory scripted lessons for grades 4, 5 & 6.
Contact: National Eating Disorders Association
603 Stewart Street, Suite 803
Seattle, WA   98101   ☎ 206-382-3587   www.nationaleatingdisorders.org

Just for Girls. Sandra Friedman. Vancouver, BC: Salal Books, 1999, 2003 (2nd edition)
Open discussion groups help girls become aware of when they are feeling fat and teach skills to
express the feelings and ideas that lie underneath. Contains session plans and handouts.
Cost is $35 (plus shipping and applicable tax).
Contact: Salal Books
#309, 101-1184 Denman Street
Vancouver, BC   V6G 2M9   ☎ + 🖷 604-689-8399
www.salal.com   salal@salal.com

Liking the Me I See in the Mirror. Suzanne Hare and Dianne Drummond.
Designed for teachers in grades 4 and higher for use with girls and boys.
Manual is $35, CD— $25, Parent Workbook—$8 (plus shipping)
Contact: Food and Nutrition Services
Grey Nuns Community Hospital
1100 Youville Drive West
Edmonton AB T6L 5X8

Preventing Eating Disorders: A Handbook of Interventions and Special Challenges.
Niva Piran, Michael P. Levine & Catherine Steiner-Adair, editors. Philadelphia, PA: Taylor
and Francis, 1999

A Quest For Health: A Toolkit For Speakers
Sheena's Place, 875 Spadina Rd., Toronto, ON   416-927-8900   www.sheenasplace.org

When Girls Feel Fat: Helping Girls Through Adolescence. Sandra Susan Friedman. Toronto,
ON: HarperCollins, 1997, 2000 (2nd edition) also Firefly Books, 2000 (US edition)

Eating Disorder Organizations

Anorexia Nervosa and Related Eating Disorders, Inc. (ANRED)
P.O. Box 5102
Eugene, OR   97405
☎ 503-344-1144   www.anred.com

National Association of Anorexia Nervosa and Associated Disorders (ANAD)
Highland Hospital
Highland Park, IL   60035
☎ 708-432-8000   www.ANAD.org

National Eating Disorders Association (formerly EDAP)
603 Stewart Street, Suite 803
Seattle, WA   98101
☎ 206-382-3587   🖷 206-382-34793   www.nationaleatingdisorders.org

National Center of Overcoming Overeating
P.O. Box 1257, Old Chelsea Station
New York, NY   10113-0920
☎ 212-875-0442   www.overcomingovereating.com

National Eating Disorder Information Centre (NEDIC)
CW 1-211, 200 Elizabeth Street
Toronto, ON   M5G 2C4
☎ 416-340-4156   1-866-633-4220   📠 416-340-4736   www.nedic.ca

Food and Nutrition

Nourishing Your Daughter: Help Your Child Develop a Healthy Relationship with Food and Her Body. Carol Beck. Perigee Books, 2001

Secrets of Feeding a Healthy Family.
Ellyn Satter. Kelcy Press, Madison, WI. 1999
1-877-844-0857   www.ellynsatter.com

Vitality Program
Health Services and Promotion
Health and Welfare Canada
Jeanne Mance Bldg., 4th floor
Ottawa, ON   K1A 1B4
☎ 613-957-8331

Gender and Female Development

Meeting at the Crossroads: Women's Psychology and Girls' Development.
Carol Gilligan & Lyn Mikel Brown. Cambridge, MA: Harvard University Press, 1992

Women's Growth in Connection: Writings from the Stone Centre.
Judith Jordan, Alexandra G. Kaplan, Jean Baker Miller, Irene P. Stiver & Janet L. Surrey, editors. New York, NY: The Guilford Press, 1991

You Just Don't Understand: Men and Women in Conversation.
Deborah Tannen. New York, NY: Ballantine Books, 1990

Media

BRANDchild: Insights into the Minds of Today's Global Kids: Understanding Their Relationship with Brand. Martin Lindstrom, Patricia B. Seybold.

The Center for Media Literacy.
Resources about the impact of advertising, violence and other media influences.
4727 Wiltshire Blvd. Suite 403
Los Angeles, CA   90010
☎ 213-931-4177   www.medialit.org

Deadly Persuasion: Why Women and Girls Must Fight the Addictive Powers of Advertising.
Jean Kilbourne. New York, NY: The Free Press, 1999

GO GIRLS™ Program (Giving Our Girls Inspiration and Resources for Lasting Self-Esteem)   Contact: National Eating Disorders Association (see page 158)

Just Think Foundation
P.O. Box 475638
San Francisco, CA   94147
☎ 415-292-2900   📠 415-292-1030
wwww.justthink.org   think@justthink.org

Media-Awareness Network. Developed by Health Canada: excellent resources and lesson plans that can be downloaded. Best website.   www.media-awareness.ca

MediaWatch (Canada) Excellent resource. Has contact addresses for writing letters.
517 Wellington St. West, Suite 204
Toronto, ON   M5V 1G1
☎ 416-408-2065   📠 416-408-2069   www.mediawatch.ca

Media Watch (U.S.) An organization dedicated to attacking sexism in advertising
PO Box 618
Santa Cruz, CA   95061-0618
☎ 408-423-6355   www.mediawatch.org

Physical Activity and Sports

Disordered Eating and Athletes: The Facts.
Promoting Positive Body Image and Preventing Disordered Eating in Athletes: Tips and Strategies.
The Bodysense Basics: Promoting Positive Body Image and Preventing Disordered Eating in Sports.
Contact: BODYSENSE   attn: Heidi Mack
www.bodysense.ca   bodysense@pinecrest-queensway.com

The Bodywise Woman: Reliable Information about Physical Activity and Health. 1990
The Melpomene Institute
1010 University Avenue
St. Paul MN   55104
☎ 612-642-1951   📠 612-642-1871

CAAWS (Canadian Association for the Advancement of Women in Sport & Physical Activity)
N202-801 King Edward Avenue
Ottawa, ON   K1N 6N5
☎ 613-652-5667   www.caaws.ca   caaws@caaws.ca

Girls in Action....Speaking Out [Video, Leader's Guide and Peer Facilitator's Guide]
Girls and Boys in Elementary Physical Education, Issues and Action
(CAHPERD) Canadian Association for Health, Physical Activity, Recreation & Dance
403-2197 Riverside Drive
Ottawa, ON   K1H 7X3
☎ 613-523-1348   1-800-663-8708   www.cahperd.ca   info@capherd.ca

The Girl and the Game: A History of Women's Sport in Canada.
M. Ann Hall. Broadview Press, 2002

Girls on the Move: An Active Living Alphabet. (for young girls)
June E. LeDrew. Johnson Gorman Publishers. 2002   www. Jgbooks.com

Go Girls: Healthy Bodies Healthy Minds Program
(OPHEA) Ontario Physical and Health Education Association
1185 Eglinton Avenue E., Suite 501
Toronto, ON   M3C 3C6
☎ 416-426-7120   🖷 416-426-7373
www.ophea.net   info@ophea.net

On the Move: Increasing Participation of Girls and Women in Physical Activity & Sport.
Program encourages participation of girls who are not usually active in physical activity.
Contact: CAAWS and/or proMOTION plus

Play Like a Girl: A Celebration of Women in Sports.
Sue Macy & Jane Gottesman. New York: Henry Holt and Company, Inc, 1999

Premier's Sport Awards Program Resources and Active Schools Manual
Contact: JW Sporta
        #228 – 1367 West Broadway Avenue
        Vancouver, BC   V6H 4A9
        ☎ 604-738-2468   🖷 604-737-6043
        www.psap.jwsporta.ca   psap@jwsporta.ca

proMOTION plus: Girls and Women in Physical Activity and Sport
#305-1367 West Broadway
Vancouver, BC   V6H 4A9
☎ 604-738-7175   🖷 604-737-3075
www.promotionplus.org   info@promotionplus.org

Promoting Fitness and Self-Esteem in Your Overweight Child. Teresa Pitman & Miriam
Kaufman, MD. Toronto, ON: HarperPerennial, 1994   (Firefly Books, 2000)

Women's Sports Foundation
Eisenhower Park
East Meadow, New York   11554
☎ 516-542-4700   🖷 516-542-4716   wosport@aol.com

Raising Our Athletic Daughters: How Sports can Build Self-Esteem and Save Girls' Lives.
J. Zimmerman & G. Reavill. New York: Doubleday, 1998

FILM/VIDEO

BEAUTY AND THE BEACH   53 minutes
Produced by Cinefocus
Video draws parallels between historical changes in women's position in Western society and changes in the swimsuit. While celebrating the liberation of the female the video calls attention to the contradictions in the decreasing size of the swimsuit.
Contact: Filmakers Library
      124 East 40th St.
      New York, NY   10016
      ☎ 212 808 4980
      www.filmakers.com   info@filmakers.com

BEYOND KILLING US SOFTLY: The Strength To Resist 33 minutes
Jean Kilbourne film. This film presents leading authors in the fields of the psychology of girls and women, eating disorders, gender studies, violence against women and media literacy and focuses their ideas on practical solutions and the best tactics for reclaiming our female culture.
Contact: Cambridge Documentary Films
      PO Box 390385
      Cambridge, MA   02139
      ☎ 617-484-3393   617-484-0754   cdf@shore.net

BEYOND THE LOOKING GLASS 28 minutes
Grade 8-10 teacher resource (can be used for younger girls). Focuses on self-esteem, thoughts, feelings, identification of attitudes, stereotypes, body image and provides direction to garner support for problem solving. Produced in the U.S.
Contact: McIntyre Media
      30 Kelfield Street
      Rexdale, ON M9W 5A1
      ☎ 1-800-565-3036   416-245-8660

BODY IMAGE   30 minutes
Half hour program designed to separate media hype from reality, to help young people learn to make right choices and develop an effective, healthy lifestyle. (Grades 6-10)
Contact: Heartland Releasing
      1102- 8th Avenue, 3rd Floor
      Regina, SK S4R 1C9
      ☎ 306-777-0888   306-586-3537

BREAKING SIZE PREJUDICE   23 minutes
Developed by Mary Kay Wardlaw, MS. University of Wyoming.
An education video to promote body-size acceptance for youth aged 11 to 17 years.
Contact: UW FCS Department
      Attention: WIN Wyoming
      P.O. Box 3353
      Laramie, WY   82071
      ☎ 307-766-5375   307-766-5686   studer@uwyo.edu

IS IT REALLY ME? How Teenage Girls View Their Bodies   30 minutes
Brenda Siemer and Emma Morris, Sister Production
Ten young women share their insecurities with their bodies while taking a dancing class with Ann Reinking and Gwen Verdon, veterans of the Broadway stage and guest who encourage them to focus on their inner selves and express feelings through movement.
Contact: Filmakers Library   [see *Beauty and the Beach* above]

KILLING US SOFTLY: ADVERTISING'S IMAGE OF WOMEN [1979] 28 minutes
Produced by: Cambridge Documentary Films
American feminist Jean Kilbourne casts a critical eye on the power and influence of advertising.
Distributor: National Film Board of Canada (catalog # 0179 389) [see also *Beyond Killing Us Softly*]

KILLING US SOFTLY 3   34 minutes
Contact: Media Education Foundation
      26 Center St.
      Northampton, MA   01060
      ☎ 1-800-659-6882
      www.mediaed.org   mediaed@meidaed.org

SCANNING TELEVISION: VIDEOS FOR MEDIA LITERACY IN CLASS
Four one-hour videos plus Video Teacher's Guide. Copyright-cleared video excerpts that allow teachers to use real media while teaching media literacy.
Contact: Harcourt and Brace Canada
      55 Horner Avenue
      Toronto, ON   M8Z 4X6
      ☎ 1-800-387-7278

SLIM HOPES: MEDIA'S OBSESSION WITH THINNESS [1995] 29 minutes
Another Jean Kilbourne film excellent for high school. (see also *Still Killing Us Softly 3*)
Contact: Kinetic Video Inc.
      409 Dundas East
      Toronto, ON   M5A 2A5
      ☎ 416-963-5979   1-800-263-6910   ⊟ 416-925-0653

STILL KILLING US SOFTLY [1987] 30 minutes
Produced by: Cambridge Documentary Films (see also *Beyond Killing Us Softly*)
This sequel to Killing Us Softly offers tools for developing a critical approach to mass media.
Distributor: National Film Board of Canada (catalog # 0187 145)

TAKE ANOTHER LOOK [1994] 24 min
Produced by: Lisa O'Brien and Bernice Vanderlaan
This film is a dramatic fantasy on self-esteem for viewers aged 11-13. It encourages discussion on self-esteem, body image, the beauty and diet industries, self-respect and the need for peer support.
Distributor: McNabb and Connolly (as above)

YOUR NAME IN CELLULITE [1995]   6 minutes
A film by Gail Noonan.
A wickedly funny satire about the disparity between a woman's natural beauty and the ideal promoted by the mega-billion dollar advertising industry. Visit their website for information on "The Girls Project" which celebrates young women's lives around the world.
Contact: Women Make Movies
           462 Broadway, Suite 500K
           New York NY   10013
           ☎ 212-925-0606
           www.wmm.com   orders@wmm.com

WEBSITES

About-Face – [A San Francisco based organization committed to promoting positive body image and self-esteem in girls and women.]   www.about-face

Adios Barby – wicked and true.   www.Adios.Barby.com

*Body Positiv*e – size acceptance web site.   www.bodypositive.com

The Body Positive – empowers youth to celebrate their real shape instead of what society promotes as the ideal body.   www.thebodypostive.org

Bullying – site developed by students.   www.bullying.org

Femina – sites for, by and about women: Includes Cybergrrl-building communities online for women and girls.   www.femina.cybergrrl.com

Girls, Inc. – national organization dedicated to helping every girl become strong, smart and bold. Educational programs and activities.   www.girlsinc.org

Girl Power – national public education campaign to help, encourage and motivate 9-14 year old girls to make the most of their lives.   www.health.org/gpower

Mind on The Media – independent thinking and fostering critical analysis of the media message.   www.mindonthemedia.org

Smart Girl – written by teenage girls who visit the site.   www.smartgirl.com

Something Fishy – the most comprehensive web site for eating disorders.
                www.somethingfishy.org

Teen Health – hundreds of articles and Q & A on keeping fit and healthy, body, mind and soul. (Excellent site)   www.teenshealth.org

NOTES:

JUST FOR GIRLS
Vancouver: Salal Books, 2003   ISBN# 0-9698883-5-X   176 pages $35.00

The newly revised second edition of this manual contains the blueprint for the *JUST FOR GIRLS* program, 18 structured session plans and 25 reproducible handouts. The program is a discussion group program that looks at what 'feeling fat' means to girls, teaches them skills to decode the *language of fat*, and encourages them to tell the stories and express the feelings that lie underneath. It helps girls understand the societal pressures that they face during adolescence and the physical and emotional changes they are experiencing. It teaches girls how to strengthen their friendships and support one another.

WHEN GIRLS FEEL FAT Helping Girls Through Adolescence
Toronto: HarperCollins, 2000   ISBN# 0-00-638609-1   270 pages $19.95 ($14.95 US)

Sandra Friedman's friendly guide helps adults (and girls) understand and cope with the difficult process of adolescence. It demystifies the relationships girls have with their body image, sexuality, eating disorders, friends, parents, school and the media. *WHEN GIRLS FEEL FAT* gives parents, teachers and other professionals clear and proven strategies to deal with conflict, to recognize how 'worries about weight' can lead to serious eating disorders, and to maintain a connection with girls in the face of their 'tuning out'.

BODY THIEVES Help Girls Reclaim their Natural Bodies and Become Physically Active
Vancouver, Salal Books, 2002   ISBN# 0-9698883-3-3   264 pages $19.95 ($14.95 US)

BODY THIEVES addresses what happens to girls in the process of growing up that silences their voices and holds them hostage to the bathroom scale at the expense of their self-esteem. It looks at how parents, teachers, coaches and mentors can implement prevention strategies in the context of girls' lives and experiences. It examines the barriers to girls' being physically active and provides the reader with practical suggestions to raise healthy, active girls of all shapes and sizes.

Visit www.salal.com for additional information concerning Sandra Friedman's professional training workshops, public information seminars, and consulting services.

____ X   **NURTURING GIRLPOWER** (2003)   ISBN 0-9698883-4-1 $35.00 $_____

____ X   **JUST FOR GIRLS** (2003)   ISBN 0-9698883-5-X $35.00   _____

____ X   **BODY THIEVES** (2002)   ISBN 0-9698883-3-3 $19.95/us$14.95   _____

____ X   **WHEN GIRLS FEEL FAT** (2000)   ISBN 0-00-638609-1 $19.95/us$14.95   _____

____ X   book(s)   *Free shipping for US$ orders*   shipping @ $3/book within Canada   +_____

____   *Canadian residents only add 7% GST (or 15% HST in postal codes A, B & E)*   +_ _ _ _ _ _

Ship to: TOTAL: $_____

NAME:_____

AGENCY:_____POSITION:_____

STREET ADDRESS:_____

CITY:_____ PROV / STATE:_____ POSTAL CODE:_____

TELEPHONE:_____wk / home FAX:_____ e-MAIL:_____

VISA / MASTERCARD #_____ expiry:_____ /_____

SALAL BOOKS #309, 101-1184 Denman Street, Vancouver, BC, Canada   V6G 2M9
☎+ 🖷 604-689-8399   salal@salal.com